I0009571

Nikon Z50 II Guidebook

A Complete Manual for Photographers and Videographers to Unlock Expert Tips, Pro-Level Techniques, and Advanced Features for Producing Attractive Shots

Tim Elvis

GENERAL OVERVIEW
THE NIKON Z50 II DISCOVERY

Nikon's latest APS-C digital camera, the Z50II, is ideal for beginners. Its CMOS sensor is 21MP. It is made especially for picture and video shooters who desire a tiny camera that is easy to share, much like the original Z50. The most of the changes are on the video side of the camera, although it does have better AF and better burst modes than the previous one.

About Essential requirements

- 20.9MP APS-C sensor
- Twin control dials
- Full-width 4K video up to 30p (60p with crop)
- 3D-tracking autofocus and subject recognition for nine subject types
- Up to 11fps mechanical, with up to 1 second pre-release capture
- Fully articulated 3.2" touchscreen
- Single UHS-II SD card slot in battery compartment
- 2.36M dot EVF with brightness up to 1000nits

Important and Novel Features

As the name implies, the Z50II is an upgraded model of the company's first APS-C Z-mount camera. Most of its improvements are due to the inclusion of a more recent, powerful Expeed 7 CPU, although there are a few other minor but potentially significant modifications as well.

Picture Control Button and Adaptable Color Picture Control

Now, the Z50II has a dedicated "Picture Control" button that allows you to choose the color setting of the camera. This modification helps clarify what it is and who it is for, but it has nothing to do with processing speed. Buttons now have new names, but that's not the only change. The first model with "flexible" Picture Control profiles—which let you to download more profiles or update existing ones—is the Z50II. To prevent it from becoming too much, you may add additional and choose which ones appear when you touch the Picture Control button. The camera has 31. Nikon is one of the few manufacturers that allows you to choose between the built-in modes, at least since 2008. You may modify the Picture Controls by adding your own unique tone curve or adjusting the brightness and sharpness of the profile using the company's NX Studio program. However, unlike with a LUT, you can only alter the overall hue; you cannot remap colors. This implies that your ability to influence how the colors react is restricted. We anticipate that the majority of users will test out the capability that allows them to download settings for the Creator Recipe from Nikon's Imaging Cloud.

A viewfinder with more clarity

Furthermore, the Z50II has a viewfinder that is twice as brilliant as the previous version, with a maximum brightness of 1000 nits. The display is not bright enough to properly evaluate HLG high dynamic range capture, while maintaining the same 2.36M dot resolution.

Recognition of subjects and 3D tracking

One of the most significant improvements made by the new engine is the Z50II's auto-focus technology. It can now recognize nine subjects instead of just three since it inherits the topic recognition modes from other recent Nikon cameras.

	Nikon Z50II	Nikon Z50 / Zfc
Subjects recognized	• Humans (Eye, Face, Upper Body) • Birds • Cats • Dogs • Cars • Motorcycles • Bicycles • Trains • Airplanes	• Humans (Eye, Face, Upper Body) • Cats • Dogs

The 3D Tracking AF mode, which speeds up tracking objects even if the camera hasn't been taught to detect them, is another feature.

Pre-burst and C30

The Z50II can shoot at fast speeds in e-shutter mode, another Expeed 7 function, which allows you to start buffering photographs before the shutter button is half-pressed and save images captured up to one second before the shutter button is completely depressed. The Z50II can shoot at up to 30 frames per second or 15 frames per second with tracking in its C30 and C15 modes; however it can only store JPEGs.

The Nikon Imaging Cloud

The Z50II is compatible with Nikon's Imaging Cloud service, which was introduced with the Z6III. It may automatically submit your photos to Nikon's servers when connected to a Wi-Fi network. Any third-party cloud storage provider, such as Dropbox, Google Drive, or Lightroom, may then receive them. You may configure your camera to sync Picture Control settings from your phone or computer and download software updates automatically to keep it current. Similar functions are included in many cameras, but in order to utilize them, you must couple them with a smartphone or another camera. On the other hand, when connected to your computer, the Z50II may function independently.

What's innovative with video?

Nikon has made significant improvements to video even though it still uses the same sensor as the Z50. The Z50II can now encode video with an accuracy of 10 bits. This enables it to record video in HLG for HDR playback on TVs and displays or N-Log for the optimum color and tone grading. The Z50II can now capture 4K/60 video from a limited area of the sensor. Additionally, according to Nikon, electronic image stabilization (eVR) in video mode is more steady and superior. Additionally, vloggers may utilize the Z50II's "product review" focusing mode to discuss a particular product. If an item is held up in front of the camera, this mode may be utilized in place of face recognition AF.

Handling and body

 The body of this camera is quite similar to that of its predecessor. In other words, it resembles a somewhat scaled-down model of Nikon's original Z-series full-frame cameras. Despite the smaller size, the Z50II still has a decent hand grip. The majority of the body is made of fiber-reinforced plastic. Because of this, it feels substantial without being too hefty. The camera is comfortable and safe to grasp thanks to its rough texture on the handgrip and rear corner. To utilize the forward and back command buttons with your fingers and thumb, you don't need to move your hand from where it is on the camera.

 It has four extra buttons on the rear of the camera than its predecessor. The controls are much more similar to those of full-frame Z models thanks to these four additional buttons, plus and minus zoom buttons, a drive mode button, and a "DISP" button. Additionally, there is an additional button above the camera. "Picture Control," as it is known, is situated beneath the controls for [REC], ISO, and Exposure Comp. The Z50II lacks the full-frame versions' joystick, and its top plate houses the Stills/Movie switch that the full-frame models have around their DISP buttons. The Play and Drive Mode buttons are positioned incorrectly in comparison to the full-frame variants. For this adjustment to be apparent, we don't believe many users will attempt to take pictures of both cameras simultaneously. Like the Zfc and Z30, the Z50II also has a screen that can move in all directions instead of tilting up and down. The fact that Nikon has changed this is not surprising, considering all four of its APS-C Z-mount models have been referred to as "creators."

Viewfinder and screen

The Z50II's viewfinder is twice as bright as the previous model's, with a maximum brightness of 1000 nits. When you're using the camera outdoors in the sun, this should help your eyes adapt. However, it lacks sufficient brightness to adequately preview HLG images. Given the Z50II's low position in the range, the 2.36M dot display still has a poor resolution. In other words, for a camera this inexpensive, its 0.68x zoom is rather large.

About Ports and slots

These Z50II stats demonstrate the progress made since the first model was released five years ago. Its USB connector has been upgraded to Type C for 5Gbit/s transfer speeds, and it can now fully use the faster UHS-II cards in its SD card slot. Additionally, it is compatible with the UVC/UAC USB video and audio standards, so you don't need any additional software or drivers to use it as a camera. The camera is now considerably more useful as a video camera since it incorporates an ear jack for tracking sound.

A battery

The new EN-EL25a battery that powers the Z50II has a 9.4Wh capacity rather than an 8.5Wh one. Despite this 10% increase, the Z50II's CIPA battery rates are 250 shots with the rear screen and 230 shots with the viewfinder. The powerful CPU is probably the reason they are about 20% less expensive than the previous generation. Given that CIPA figures usually anticipate significant flash use and more shot review than most users really do, we wouldn't be shocked to get twice as many shots as this in our own usage—more if we were shooting bursts. You can obtain roughly 9% more pictures when power-saving mode is enabled, but these aren't very good stats for a camera you may use often. The camera's USB-C connector allows charging, making it simple to recharge the battery. Nevertheless, a charger is not included.

Early impressions

Some people believe that the Z50II is just marginally superior over the Z50. It doesn't contribute anything new and has the same sensor in a comparable body. It lacks any characteristics that are entirely novel for its class or that challenge our preconceived notions about what photography is capable of. It's okay. The Z50II is the camera of choice for many individuals purchasing their first camera. The Z50II, which accomplishes the essentials well without breaking the bank, would have been ideal for me when I first began shooting photos. For the day I had it, the Z50II was excellent for shooting; nothing about it seemed flimsy. I never felt like I had to wait for the camera or that it couldn't shoot fast enough to capture what I aimed it at because of its excellent build quality, handling, and speed given its size. The focussing was one notable aspect. Nikon's 3D tracking technology and subject identification are as strong in the Z50II as they were in the Z50. Finding focusing systems for novice cameras used to be challenging since inexperienced users need the greatest assistance. However, the best systems are also the priciest; therefore they are not included in less costly cameras. That is not how the Z50II operates.

I felt secure using the Z50II's focusing system, even in automatic subject identification mode. Better more, it locates the subject on its own, saving you the trouble while you're rushing to capture the moment. That would be wonderful for pet owners who want to showcase their fast-moving dogs and cats without going over budget, or for parents who want to snap a nice photo of their kids enjoying sports. Additionally, there are so many video features that Nikon seems to be targeting both content creators and first-year film students. The standard 4K resolution will be sufficient for novice photographers who also want to film video. They won't be able to employ functions like N-Log or waveforms, however. The Picture Control button comes next. Camera manufacturers tend to believe that color profiles are the greatest approach to encourage more people to take pictures, but I'm not sure. For instance, Fujifilm unveiled two cameras with film modeling knobs this year, while Panasonic unveiled its LUT button.

Many people want color customization, but since Nikon's system is round-based, it may be difficult for novices to grasp. Instead of sending pictures directly from your phone to your camera, you choose the ones you want using Nikon's app, and your camera then sends them via Wi-Fi. I am aware that there may be some misunderstandings since the camera must be online on its own. I have years of experience in tech support. One major issue that no one likes to discuss is lenses. For its APS-C systems, the business produces four zooms with maximum apertures of 3.5 or higher and one prime lens. Although there are some excellent Sigma DC DN Contemporaries and other third-party auto focus primes available, you will need to choose a bulky and more costly Nikon full-frame alternative if you want a zoom with a fast or steady aperture.

For whom is this camera intended? (Beginners, Enthusiasts and Experts)

Beginners: An Easy Way to Get Started with Photography and Videography

For those who are new to photography and video, the Nikon Z50 II is an excellent starting point. The controls are straightforward and easy to use, making it simple to pick up and begin shooting right away. Setting the camera's ISO, shutter speed, and aperture is made simple by its guided shooting modes, which include auto and scene modes. In this manner, novices may concentrate on composition and framing while the camera handles the technical aspects. The Z50 II is convenient to take about due to its compact size and low weight. This is particularly useful if you're just starting out and want to experiment with various sorts of locations for your shots. This camera bag fits neatly into most backpacks or bags, so you don't need to carry a large one. You may carry it with you wherever you go. You may experiment with more complex settings as you improve, even though the Z50 II is designed for novices. Its fast auto focus system and excellent 20.9 MP sensors let beginners to produce crisp, detailed photos and films without needing to immediately master complex techniques. Furthermore, the camera can capture 4K video, which makes it simple for anybody wishing to start a vlog or create their own movies to produce high-quality content.

Enthusiasts: Adaptability to Creative Authority

For enthusiasts of photography and videography who are already proficient with a camera but want to further their knowledge, the Nikon Z50 II is ideal. It is simple to operate because to its sophisticated features and manual controls. Its movable knobs and photo controls make it simple to experiment with innovative in-camera filters or change the exposure settings. The Z50 II not only provides outstanding image quality but also allows users to make their own original films and images. The camera's sophisticated focusing mechanism, which combines Eye-Detection AF and fast-tracking to maintain subjects' sharpness even in highly moving settings, will also appeal to fans. This makes it ideal for shooting action pictures, portraits, and more. Filmmakers also greatly benefit from being able to capture 4K UHD video with complete pixel readout, which produces crisp, high-quality footage that can be further enhanced in post-production. For creative projects or on-the-go shots, the Z50 II's Wi-Fi and Bluetooth connection provide enthusiasts a convenient method to exchange images or manage the camera remotely. With this camera, you can push the boundaries of your creativity whether you're shooting for social media, creating content for personal projects, or exploring with sophisticated settings.

Experts: Small, dependable, and prepared for backup tasks

The Nikon Z50 II is a great choice for professional photographers or filmmakers that want a portable backup or travel camera, even if it is not a full-fledged professional camera like the Z6 or Z7. Professionals often want compact, portable cameras that maintain performance, and the Z50 II is the ideal solution for this demand. With a 20.9 MP sensor that captures crisp, detailed images for street, landscape, and headshot photography, its picture quality is more than enough for professional work. For employees who want a camera that can function in a range of environments without the weight of larger equipment, it's a fantastic option. The camera is also ideal for creating professional material because of its 4K video recording features, which include high-quality audio. The Z50 II provides the dependability and durability required for regular commercial usage, although maybe lacking the comprehensive feature set of more expensive versions. Its tiny form factor makes it easier to utilize in more dynamic, fast-paced shooting circumstances, such events or on-location shots, while its weather-sealed body guarantees that it can withstand the elements. The Z50 II's ability to work with Z-mount lenses or the ability to utilize FTZ adapters with earlier DSLR lenses gives pros that now use Nikon lenses more configuration options.

CHAPTER ONE
THE NIKON Z50 II: STARTING OFF

Initial Configuration

- Gently remove the Nikon Z50 II from the box. The camera body, lens (if purchased as a kit), battery, charger, and a few wires are all within the box. Make sure you have everything you need to set up before continuing.
- **Insert the Battery:** Insert the battery into the battery compartment located at the bottom of the camera, often next to the tripod attachment. Verify that the provided battery is inserted correctly by examining the markings within the chamber. Don't open the lid.
- **Insert the Memory Card:** The memory card slot is located next to the battery location. After opening it, insert an SD card (UHS-I or UHS-II is preferable for speed). Verify that the card is positioned correctly and that it clicks into position. To save your photos and videos, you must do this.
- **Attach the Lens:** Remove the lens from its box and remove any protective covers if the camera comes with one. Align the lens with the camera body's lens mount. Verify that the mark on the camera and the white dot on the lens match. Slowly rotate the lens counterclockwise until it snaps into position.

Primary Power-On and Language Configuration

- **Turn on the Camera:** To turn on the camera, flick the power switch to the "ON" position once the lens and batteries have been attached. The first configuration option ought to appear when the camera's screen illuminates.
- **Choose Your Language:** The first thing the camera will do is prompt you to choose your language. Use the buttons or touchscreen to choose the language that is most convenient for you. English will thereafter be the primary language used by the camera for its settings and display.
- Configure the Time and Date you will then be prompted to choose the time and date. If you want to arrange your pictures and videos according to the date they were shot, this is crucial. To adjust the time, date, and time zone, utilizes the dial and lines on the camera. Setting the correct time and date is crucial, particularly if you want to utilize GPS or geotagging.

Important Add-ons for the Nikon Z50 II

Extra batteries and a grip for batteries

Although the Nikon Z50 II is renowned for having a somewhat long battery life, it may soon run out of power when used often, particularly when recording video or shooting constantly, like most cameras. To avoid running out of power in the midst of a shoot, you should get additional batteries. The Z50 II is powered by a portable EN-EL25 battery. You may avoid waiting by keeping a few spares on hand. For longer projects or if you want to perform a lot of on-location photography, you may also wish to get a battery grip. This accessory facilitates holding the camera, particularly while you're shooting for extended periods of time, and it often includes additional battery parts to extend the battery's charge.

UHS-I or UHS-II flash drives

For every camera, a reliable and fast memory card is essential for storing your picture and video information. The Nikon Z50 II is compatible with SD UHS-I and UHS-II cards. Faster writing rates on UHS-II cards are useful for snapping a lot of photos rapidly or recording 4K video. For most individuals, UHS-I cards will still function well if money is limited. The process of transferring data to your computer might be accelerated with UHS-II cards. To guarantee seamless functioning and enough space, it is advised that you buy many high-capacity memory cards (at least 64GB or 128GB). During a shoot, you may keep a large number of images and films in this manner without constantly switching cards.

Lens filters (polarizer, ND, and UV)

Lens filters are a simple and efficient solution to enhance your images and videos while adding additional protection for your lens. **These are a few of the more significant kinds:**

- UV Filters: These filters preserve picture quality while shielding the lens from moisture, dust, and scratches. When filming outdoors in inclement weather, they are really beneficial.
- Neutral Density (ND) Filters: By reducing the amount of light entering the lens, ND filters assist you in managing exposure. When photographing in the daylight, they are excellent for maintaining the proper exposure, particularly when using larger apertures or slower shutter speeds. When filming, ND filters may be used to control motion blur.

↓ Polarizing Filters: By reducing glare and reflections from items like glass or water, these filters make the sky seem more saturated, which improves contrast in your outdoor photos. They are essential for everyone who takes photographs of the natural world.

Monopod or Tripod

Whether you're photographing landscapes, portraits, or video, a tripod is one of the most essential items you can own. Your camera will not shake if you keep it steady, allowing you to snap time-lapse or long exposure pictures without blur. It's also necessary if you want to create steady videos or blog. A monopod is a choice for those who want something smaller and more portable. Compared to a tripod, it is more portable and yet offers security for certain kinds of photography, particularly in crowded or fast-paced areas.

An external microphone

The built-in microphone on the Nikon Z50 II is good for short films, but if you want to create high-quality videos or blog often, you need acquire a second microphone. Your films will sound more polished if you use external microphones to capture sound much more clearly and reduce background noise. Because it captures sound from the front and eliminates noise from the sides, a shotgun microphone is an excellent choice for general usage. If you often conduct interviews or need a microphone with multidirectional pickup, take into consideration a lavalier (lapel) microphone. Both kinds of microphones may be connected to the camera via the 3.5mm mic connector.

Camera Bag

Keeping your camera, lenses, memory cards, and other equipment secure during travel and storage requires a camera bag or backpack. Choose a bag with plenty of compartments and cushioning to shield your equipment from scuffs and scratches. Select an easy-to-carry bag with supple straps if you want to shoot photos outdoors or while traveling. When you're shooting in public, you may avoid calling attention to yourself by using camera bags that are designed to seem like ordinary bags.

Lens cap and screen protector

A screen cover is an inexpensive but essential purchase to prevent scratches, smudging, and other damage to your camera's LCD screen. The Z50 II's touchscreens are simple to use, and a screen protector will eventually keep the screen clean and scratch-free.

Another essential tool for shielding the lens from dust, grime, and scratches while not in use is a lens cap. You can maintain your lens in excellent condition by investing a little amount of money on this.

The Remote Shutter Release

A remote shutter release will be helpful to those who like taking close-ups or landscape photos. By taking photos without touching the camera, you can reduce the possibility of camera shaking and blurry images. A self-portrait or a long exposure are excellent instances of this as even the slightest movement may ruin the picture. You may choose between a wired and Wi-Fi version based on your demands.

External Speedlight or Flash

The Nikon Z50 II's illumination is inadequate for professional photography, even with its built-in flash. An external flash or speedlight gives you greater control over the lighting, allowing you to take more vibrant and well-lit photos, particularly in low light conditions. Features of external flashes include TTL (Through the Lens) metering, which automatically adjusts the flash output depending on the exposure settings of the image, and bounce flash, which disperses the light for softer, more natural illumination.

The Cleaning Kit

A camera cleaning kit is one of the most crucial items you may own to maintain the condition of your equipment. The lens and sensor must be kept clean to preserve picture quality. Lens wipes, a microfiber cloth, and a lens brush are often included in a basic package. For a more thorough cleaning, you would require a sensor cleaning kit. It enables you to safely and gently clear the camera's sensor of dust.

Compatible Lenses

Nikon Z DX 16-50mm VR Lens (Kit Lens) f/3.5-6.3

The Nikon Z DX 16-50mm f/3.5-6.3 VR lens was included with the Nikon Z50 II since it was most likely purchased as a kit. The focal length of this compact, flexible zoom lens is equivalent to that of a full-frame 24–75mm lens, making it ideal for daily photography. This makes it an excellent lens for close-ups as well as wide-angle photos (such as of buildings and landscapes).

Important Features

- Its broad zoom range makes it ideal for a variety of images, including candid portraits and landscapes.
- **Compact and light:** It won't add weight to your gear and is convenient to carry.
- **Vibration Reduction (VR):** This function keeps the camera stable, which is useful for handheld photos taken in low light.
- **Affordable:** For the kit lens, it's an excellent value that doesn't significantly degrade picture quality.

The Nikon Z 50mm f/1.8 S Lens

The Z 50mm f/1.8 S is among the top prime lenses for the Nikon Z50 II. Its normal focal length makes it ideal for street photography, portraiture, and even tasks requiring low light levels. Because it produces lovely bokeh (blurred backdrop) and makes it simple to distinguish the subject from the background, the f/1.8 aperture is a favorite among photographers who like shooting with short depth of focus.

Important Features

- **A wide aperture (f/1.8):** This produces stunning bokeh and is excellent for low light photography.
- **Sharp and clear images:** It is renowned for having excellent image quality throughout the frame.
- Because of its quick focusing, it works well for both still and motion pictures.
- **Compact size:** The Z50 II body has no added mass, making it portable.

Because it can deliver professional-quality photos without breaking the bank, this lens is ideal for anybody who wants to capture photographs.

Nikon Z DX 18-140mm f/3.5-6.3 VR Lens

The Nikon Z DX 18-140mm f/3.5-6.3 VR lens is a fantastic alternative for those who like a wider range of lenses than the 16-50mm lens. It may be utilized for a greater variety of shooting scenarios, including landscapes, buildings, photos, and animals, thanks to its extended zoom range. With a focal length of 28-210mm, the 18-140mm lens is ideal for those who desire a more versatile zoom lens without having to constantly switch lenses.

Important Features

- The broad zoom range (28–210mm) makes it ideal for vacation photography and capturing a variety of subjects, such as distant animals or expansive landscapes.
- As the name implies, vibration reduction (VR) keeps handheld photographs stable when the lens length is greater.
- **Affordable:** For those on a tight budget who nevertheless need a versatile lens that can be used for a variety of shooting styles, this one is ideal.

This lens is a fantastic balance of quality, cost, and versatility, and it can be used in a variety of situations.

The Nikon Z 24-70mm f/2.8 S Lens

For enhancing your photography, the Nikon Z 24-70mm f/2.8 S lens is the ideal option. Its visual quality and performance are excellent. The f/2.8 aperture allows you to capture stunning subject separation and bokeh even in low light. The 24-70mm lens length range is the "bread-and-butter" range for a lot of seasoned photographers. It is ideal for weddings, parties, landscapes, and portraits.

Important Features

- **Fast constant aperture (f/2.8):** Ideal for creative depth of field management and low light levels.
- A versatile focal range of 24 to 70 mm allows for both portraits and wide-angle photography.
- **Superior construction quality:** Made of premium materials and weather-sealed, it offers exceptional clarity and sharpness, providing high-quality images with less distortion.

For dedicated photographers who want excellent results in a variety of genres, this lens is the perfect all-around workhorse, despite being somewhat bigger and more costly.

The Nikon Z 85mm f/1.8 S Lens

An excellent choice for portrait photographers is the Nikon Z 85mm f/1.8 S. Because it provides the proper working distance and compression for a pleasing picture, the 85mm focal length is perfect for taking portraits. Beautiful bokeh, or a smooth, soft backdrop that highlights your subject, is produced with the f/1.8 aperture.

Important Features

- **Focal length:** Because it provides the ideal balance of backdrop separation and compression, 85mm is often regarded as the greatest lens for photographs.
- **Wide aperture (f/1.8):** This setting allows for a narrow depth of focus and produces lovely bokeh.
- **Outstanding picture quality:** even with the lens wide open, color and clarity are excellent.
- **Compact and lightweight:** Despite being a prime lens, it is nevertheless rather portable.

This is the lens you should get if you are serious about taking pictures and need one that performs well in both artificial and natural light.

The Nikon Z 14–30mm f/4 S Lens

The Nikon Z 14-30mm f/4 S is a great choice if you want to take images of architecture or landscapes. You have a lot of alternatives for wide-angle photos with this ultra-wide zoom lens, which has a full-frame similar focal length of 21–45mm. The f/4 aperture isn't as quick as some others, but it does a terrific job with landscape and buildings.

Important Features

- Its ultra-wide focal range (14-30mm) makes it ideal for astrophotography, architecture, and sweeping landscapes.
- It is also lightweight and compact, making it one of the smallest and lightest ultra-wide zooms for full-frame mirrorless cameras.
- Constant f/4 aperture: Provides steady performance over the zoom range.
- Sharpness and little distortion: Produces crisp, clear results even at the frame's edges.

For photographers who require wide-angle capabilities without sacrificing portability or image quality, this lens is perfect.

Sigma 56mm f/1.4 DC DN Modern Lens (For DX Format)

If you're searching for a high-quality lens designed for the DX-format (crop sensor), check out the Sigma 56mm f/1.4 DC DN Contemporary lens. Although it's not a Nikon lens, it delivers very high-quality photographs and pairs well with the Z50 II (when paired with a Z-mount adaptor). Its 56mm focal length allows you to achieve an effective full-frame equivalent focal length of around 84mm, which is ideal for low-light and portrait photography.

Important Features

- This lens is excellent for fine details and low light due to its wide f/1.4 aperture.
- **Sharpness and clarity:** Even with the lens wide open, it has excellent sharpness.
- **Affordable**: An excellent substitute for the more costly Nikon lenses that is included with the camera.

This lens is a fantastic option for photographers on a tight budget who still want the advantages of a fast aperture and excellent image quality.

Keep in mind: There are numerous lens options for the Nikon Z50 II to suit a variety of photographers, from casual hobbyists to serious photographers. With the Z-mount system, you may select a prime lens that's ideal for headshots or landscapes, a professional lens like the 24-70mm f/2.8 S, or a zoom lens like the 18-140mm that can be utilized in a variety of settings. Your choice of lens will depend on your shooting style, your budget, and the kind of job you intend to undertake. If you have a decent combination of prime and zoom lenses, you can easily capture everything from close-up portraits to expansive landscapes.

About Cases, Tripods, and Other Items

The Stability and Flexibility of Tripods

Having a tripod is one of the most essential things you can own. Even if you think you can get by without one, you'll soon realize how useful it is, particularly for landscape, long-exposure, and video shooting. The Nikon Z50 II is a lightweight, compact camera, but utilizing it with a robust tripod can help you take crystal-clear photographs, particularly in low-light or slow-shutter settings.

How to Pick the Best Tripod

When picking a tripod, the idea is to find one that meets your photography style and expectations. Here are some key elements to consider:
- Look for a tripod that can accommodate your height and adapt to various views and surface conditions. Certain tripods are ideal for limited spaces or uneven flooring because of their flexible legs.
- **Portability and Weight:** Because the Z50 II camera is small, choose a tripod that is portable as well. Despite being more costly, carbon fiber tripods are a great option if you're always on the go since they're lightweight and durable. Tripods made of aluminum are more cost-effective yet a little heavier.
- Even though the Z50 II is lightweight, use a tripod that can support more weight than you anticipated. Stability will result from this, especially in windy conditions. **The following are some fantastic choices for the Nikon Z50 II:**
  - **Manfrotto BeFree Advanced Tripod:** This lightweight and portable tripod is perfect for travel and photography in a variety of environments.
  - **Joby GorillaPod 5K:** This tripod is perfect for creative shooting and vlogging since it can be mounted to any surface or shape, including poles and tree branches.

Portable and Protective Camera Bags and Cases

A reliable camera case or backpack is crucial for safeguarding your gear, whether you're traveling or going on a picture session. Although the Nikon Z50 II is a small and robust camera, it is susceptible to dust, scratches, and impact damage if it is not properly protected. In addition to keeping your camera safe, a well-made camera bag will keep you organized, particularly if you are carrying many lenses, batteries, memory cards, and other supplies.

Selecting the Proper Camera Bag

Take into account the following characteristics while selecting a camera bag:

+ Verify the bag's dimensions to make sure it will hold your Z50 II together with any extra lenses, flashes, or accessories. It should properly fit your photography equipment and yet have space for other things, so you don't want anything too huge or too little.

+ Pick a bag with adjustable dividers or padded areas. These keep your belongings neat and prevent damage or scrapes from things crashing against one other. Additionally, some backpacks provide pockets for small accessories like external microphones, wires, and SD cards. • If you want to carry your backpack for an extended period of time, choose one with a comfortable handle or shoulder straps. Waist belts are a feature of certain backpacks for added support. **Popular choices for camera bags include:**

➢ Peak Design Everyday Bag: An adaptable, stylish, and robust bag with detachable sections that can hold any item.

➢ The Lowepro Tahoe BP 150 is a compact and lightweight camera backpack that works with mirrorless cameras such as the Z50 II. It features a straightforward design for everyday use and offers enough protection.

Lens Hoods: Better Image Quality and Protection

Although they are not necessary equipment for many photographers, lens hoods may be quite helpful, particularly for landscape and outdoor photographers. They attach to the front of your lens and aid in preventing lens flare in addition to shielding it from unforeseen bumps and scratches. When intense light sources, like the sun, reach the lens at an angle, it may cause lens flare, which can result in washed-out images and unwanted patches. By preventing some of this light from striking the lens directly, a lens hood may improve the contrast and saturation of your images.

Protecting your LCD with screen protectors

One of the main ways you'll interact with the Nikon Z50 II is via its LCD screen, especially while taking pictures, browsing menus, or editing images. But eventually, the screen might get scratched or broken. Screen protectors are a low-cost way to keep your screen safe and looking fantastic. Without compromising display quality, these thin, adhesive sheets will shield the LCD from dust, fingerprints, and scratches. They are also easy to install. If you frequently adjust your settings on the field or shoot in challenging conditions, a screen protector is extremely helpful.

Use a remote shutter release to take pictures without shaking the camera

Photographers may take pictures without physically pressing the shutter button on their camera by using a little but crucial accessory called a remote shutter release. This lessens camera shaking, which may result in blurry photos, particularly when there is little light or when the shutter speed is lowered. There are wired and wireless versions of remote shutter releases. When you don't want to touch the camera and ruin the scene, wireless versions are ideal for group portraits, astrophotography, and long-exposure photos.

Cleaning Kits for Preserving Your Gear

To get the most performance out of your camera, lenses, and other gear, you must keep them clean. Smudges, dust, and fingerprints may all obstruct your lens and sensor, resulting in blurry or unwelcome effects in your photos.

A camera cleaning kit generally contains:
- Microfiber towels for streak-free lens, screen, and other surface cleaning
- Lens brushes to remove dust or debris without harming the glass.
- Lens cleaning solution for the lens surface to get rid of oil and smudges.

When cleaning your camera equipment, always use materials designated particularly for it. Image quality may be deteriorated by common household cleaning products that might cause damage or leave residues.

Lighting and Flash Equipment: Enhancing Performance in Low Light

In some situations, the built-in flash on the Nikon Z50 II may be useful, but if you're serious about taking portraits, photographing events, or working in low light, you'll need an external flash or additional lighting gear. Compared to built-in lights, external flashes provide more power, variety, and illumination control. For more intricate lighting arrangements, you may combine many flashes, add diffusers to soften the light, or even adjust the light's direction. **The following external flashes are suggested for the Nikon Z50 II:**

- With advanced features like radio control for multi-flash setups, the Nikon SB-5000 Speedlight is a versatile, high-performance flash.
- The Godox V1 is a low-cost flash with full TTL metering functionality and a round head for softer, natural light.

Protecting Your Lenses Using Lens Caps

The lens cap is a simple but sometimes overlooked device. The lens cap shields the lens's front element while your camera is not in use. It helps keep the glass scratch-free and keeps moisture, dust, and debris off the lens. Although many lenses have their own caps, it's a good idea to include a couple spares, particularly if you change lenses often.

CHAPTER TWO
COMPREHENDING THE TECHNICAL DETAILS OF THE CAMERA

The Significance of the DX-Format Sensor

The Z50 II is one of several Nikon DSLR and mirrorless cameras that employ the DX-format sensor, a certain size image sensor. The part of the camera that captures light and transforms it into a picture is called the sensor. Despite being smaller than the FX-format (sometimes called full-frame) sensor used in more expensive cameras, the DX sensor nonetheless generates photographs of excellent quality. For comparison, a full-frame sensor is 36 x 24 mm, whereas the DX sensor is around 23.5 x 15.7 mm. This disparity in size affects the depth of focus, camera operation, and the final look of your photos.

The DX-Format's Impact on Your Photographs

The Crop Factor

One of the most important features of the DX-format sensor is its crop factor. Because the sensor is smaller than a full-frame sensor, it has a crop factor. In other words, it affects the effective focal length of your lenses. The crop factor of the Nikon Z50 II is around 1.5x. This suggests that the Z50 II's effective focal length will be 75mm when a 50mm lens is used. This results in a "cropped" field of view when compared to a full-frame camera using the same lens. When you wish to zoom in on far-off objects without using a longer lens, such in sports or wildlife photography, this might be helpful. Wide-angle photos, however, might seem a little more "zoomed in," so choose your lenses carefully when taking pictures of architecture or landscapes.

Field Depth

The depth of field in your photos is affected by the sensor's size. For creating the blurring background (bokeh) effect, a larger sensor—such as the full-frame FX sensor—allows for a greater depth of focus. More of the image will be in focus, however, since the smaller DX sensor has a larger depth of field. This could seem like a drawback if you want to isolate your subject with a creamy blur behind it, but it can really help in macro or landscape photography, when every element, from the backdrop to the foreground, has to be sharp.

Performance in Low Light

Because each pixel on a bigger sensor is larger and can capture more light, larger sensors perform better in low light and provide lower noise in photos taken at higher ISO settings. Even while it isn't as good as full-frame in very low light conditions, the DX-format sensor is nonetheless competitive, especially when compared to modern camera sensors. You may notice that your Z50 II will need higher ISO settings in low light, which means it will produce more noise (graininess) than a full-frame camera. However, this can usually be addressed rather well with the right post-processing methods or noise reduction software.

DX-Format Sensor Benefits

Cost-effectiveness

Due to their smaller size, DX-format cameras are often less costly than full-frame cameras. Because of this, the Z50 II is a compelling choice for enthusiasts, beginners, and anybody else looking for a premium mirrorless camera without having to pay the astronomical price of a full-frame body.

Small Weight and Size

If you want a camera that is portable without sacrificing picture quality, a smaller sensor makes the camera lighter and more portable. This is best shown by the Z50 II, which is small enough to be a travel camera without sacrificing quality for photos or videos.

Wide Lens Adaptability

Despite using the Z-mount system, which is typically designed for full-frame cameras, the Z50 II may still be used with a range of lenses designed for DX-format sensors in addition to full-frame lenses. You may expand your lens collection without being restricted to a certain kind thanks to its versatility. Additionally, DX lenses provide a more affordable choice for anyone looking to add additional lenses to their collection without going over budget since they are often smaller and less costly.

The DX-Format Sensor's Challenges

Limited Field of View at Wide Angles

One of the most difficult features of the DX-format sensor is the crop factor. This may lessen the effectiveness of wide-angle lenses, but it is helpful for telephoto work. A DX-format camera, such as the Z50 II, will have a smaller effective field of vision than a full-frame camera, even if a wide-angle lens may provide an amazing panoramic photo. Nikon offers wide-angle lenses tailored to the crop factor that is specifically made for DX. You may need to look for ultra-wide lenses that are compatible with the DX sensor if you want to take extremely wide landscape or architectural photos.

Less Bokeh (background blurring)

The DX-format sensor's limited ability to blur the background is another drawback. A DX-format sensor could make it harder to achieve the bokeh effect—the subtle blur behind your subject—than a full-frame camera, if you like a tight depth of focus. Though it requires a bit more planning, beautiful bokeh may still be achieved, particularly when using fast lenses with wide apertures.

The Processor EXPEED

The camera's brain is basically the EXPEED CPU. It takes care of the challenging task of processing information from the camera's sensor. The EXPEED processor transforms the raw light data collected by the image sensor during a picture shoot into the final image or video that you see. It takes care of everything, from performance speed to picture quality, so your photos and movies look fantastic. The Z50 II's EXPEED processor, which Nikon has been improving for years, is an improved model that outperforms earlier iterations in terms of usefulness and performance. The camera's whole user experience is powered by this crucial component, which is more than simply a sophisticated processor.

How Is Image Quality Affected by an EXPEED Processor?

The Nikon Z50 II is greatly impacted by the EXPEED CPU, especially when it comes to picture quality. It operates like this.
- **Noise Abatement:** Higher ISO settings might cause noise, or grainy areas in your images, especially when you're shooting in low light. Even when shooting in low light, the EXPEED processing helps to reduce noise, guaranteeing that your images are clean and sharp. This implies that you may use your camera to its full potential in dimly lit environments without sacrificing quality.
- **Accuracy of Color:** Additionally, the EXPEED processor guarantees that your photos have realistic colors. Nikon's technology helps with color reproduction, making reds, blues, and greens bright and lifelike. The colors you see in the viewfinder will be faithfully captured in the finished picture, whether you're photographing street scenes, landscapes, or portraits.

- **Range of Dynamic:** The ability of a camera to capture information in both a picture's bright highlights and dark shadows is known as its dynamic range. By making sure that details in the highlights are preserved without being blown out and that there is still enough information in the shadows to produce a balanced picture, the EXPEED processor enhances this feature. This works particularly well in photos with a lot of contrast, such sunsets or sceneries with both dark and bright elements.

How Does Performance Get Better with the EXPEED Processor?

In addition to making your photos seem better; the EXPEED CPU significantly boosts the Z50 II's speed and responsiveness. Here's how.

- **Quicker processing of images:** The camera can take and process pictures faster since the EXPEED CPU handles the laborious image processing. Particularly in burst mode, the CPU processes the picture quickly when you press the shutter button, minimizing the time between shots. Fast-paced scenarios like action or sports photography, where several images must be taken in quick succession, benefit greatly from this quick processing speed. The EXPEED processor's efficiency allows the Z50 II to shoot at up to 11 frames per second (fps) in continuous mode.

- **4K Video Capture:** ideo and still photography both need the EXPEED CPU. Up to 30 frames per second of 4K UHD footage may be recorded with the Z50 II. By quickly processing sensor data, the CPU ensures smooth and excellent video recording, producing clear, detailed footage. With the EXPEED processor, your video will appear professional whether you're vlogging, making a short film, or documenting memories. It also makes time-lapse photography and slow-motion video possible, which expands your creative possibilities.

- **Improved Tracking and Autofocus:** Additionally, the EXPEED processor improves the efficiency of the camera's autofocus feature. Phase-detection and contrast-detection autofocus are combined in the hybrid autofocus technology of the Nikon Z50 II. Faster and more accurate focusing is made possible by this, especially for moving objects or lenses with a limited depth of field. The EXPEED technology helps the camera quickly adjust focus to maintain sharp images while tracking moving objects (like animals or sports). For action photographers, this is a huge benefit since snap judgments about focus may make the difference between a beautifully captured scene and one that is fuzzy.

- **Efficiency of Batteries:** The EXPEED processor helps to optimize battery life even if its primary concentration is picture and video processing. By increasing total processing efficiency, the EXPEED processor enables the Z50 II to do tasks quickly and efficiently while using less energy during prolonged shots. In actuality, this implies that you can expect extended battery life despite the Z50 II's small size and feature set. If you are on a shoot and don't have access to a power source for charging, this is very important.

How Do You Feel About All of This?

So, as a photographer or filmmaker, what does the EXPEED processor mean to you? It essentially speeds up, optimizes, and enhances the Nikon Z50 II camera's performance. Whether you're taking still photos or videos, the processor ensures that your shots are crisp, detailed, and accurate. By automating many laborious tasks, the EXPEED processor enables novices to concentrate on composition and creativity rather than technical details. The Z50 II's enhanced performance and quicker processing speed make it an excellent instrument for both routine and more difficult activities, such event or sports photography, for both professionals and amateurs.

Compatible Lens Mount: Nikon Z-Mount

The Nikon Z-mount, a robust lens mount system designed specifically for Nikon mirrorless cameras, is used with the Nikon Z50 II. The lens mount can seem like a little detail to someone who is unfamiliar with Nikon or mirrorless cameras in general, but it's really one of the most important parts of your camera setup. Let's examine the Z-mount, how it affects your choice of lens, and how it enhances your overall shooting experience.

Describe the Z-Mount

The Z-mount, which has a larger diameter, is used by Nikon mirrorless cameras. Compared to the previous F-mount used in Nikon DSLRs, the Z-mount is bigger and has a smaller flange distance—the space between the lens and the sensor. There are several noteworthy benefits to this design, particularly with regard to lens performance and the overall weight and size of the camera system. To put it simply, the Z-mount makes it easier for lenses to perform at their best, allowing more light to reach the sensor and enabling the creation of more powerful and compact lens designs. This is particularly important for those looking for a camera system that preserves picture quality while being lighter and more portable.

Benefits of Z-Mount

+ **More light equals a larger mount diameter:** The Z-mount's wider mount diameter (55mm), which is much more than the F-mount's 44mm diameter, is one of its main advantages. This improves optical performance and creates sharper pictures with more contrast and color accuracy by letting lighter pass through the lens and into the sensor. In other words, lenses made specifically for the Z-mount can capture more light, which improves picture quality, especially in low light conditions.

- **A smaller flange distance is equivalent to Improved Lens Construction:** The Z-mount system has a 16mm shorter flange distance—the space between the camera sensor and the lens mount. More creative flexibility in lens design is made possible by the decreased distance. It is possible to make lenses lighter and smaller without sacrificing functionality. Additionally, it makes it easier for Nikon and other manufacturers to produce lenses with faster apertures (f/1.4 or f/1.8) without sacrificing optimal performance. This gives photographers a wider range of lenses to choose from, especially if they want lenses that generate stunning bokeh (blurred background) or work well in low light.
- **Improved Autofocus Capability:** Nikon's Z-series cameras, notably the Z50 II, offer quicker and more precise focusing due to the larger mount and shorter flange distance. Whether you're shooting action or swiftly moving animals, it's easier to concentrate on moving objects since autofocus motors operate more effectively when the lens and sensor are closer together. When smooth focus is needed for dynamic images during video recording, this feature is very helpful.

Z-Mount lens compatibility

Since the Z-mount was specifically designed for Nikon's mirrorless system, it works flawlessly with all Z-mount lenses. With choices spanning from wide-angle to telephoto and macro, Nikon's Z-mount lens lineup is growing, offering a great deal of adaptability for a range of shooting styles. These lenses provide better picture quality and performance since they are designed for the new mirrorless system. **An overview of the types of Z-mount lenses you may come across is provided below:**

- **Conventional prime lenses:** These lenses are known for their outstanding bokeh and clarity, and they have fixed focal lengths. One great example is the Nikon Z 50mm f/1.8 S, which is great for taking portraits, taking pictures in low light, and producing beautiful background blur.
- **Lenses with Wide Angles:** Wide-angle lenses like the Nikon Z 14-30mm f/4 S are very useful for landscape and architectural photographers. Large-scale scene capture and clarity are two of these lenses' best qualities.
- **Lenses for Telephoto:** The Nikon Z 70-200mm f/2.8 VR S is one example of a telephoto lens that can capture far-off scenes with amazing clarity. Their narrow

depth of focus and ability to isolate the subject effectively make them ideal for portrait, sports, and wildlife photography.

- **Large-scale lenses:** A great option for taking close-up pictures of flowers, insects, or other little details is the Nikon Z 105mm f/2.8 VR S. These lenses provide a strong focus on very tiny targets and are designed for incredibly detailed close-up photography.

Using Z-Mount Cameras with F-Mount Lenses

The Z-mount system's backward compatibility with Nikon's older F-mount lenses—the ones that work with DSLR cameras—is among its most alluring features. You may use almost any F-mount lens with your Z50 II thanks to Nikon's FTZ converter (F-to-Z mount adapter). If you already have a collection of F-mount lenses and are switching from a Nikon DSLR, this is a huge advantage. **But there are a few things to think about:**

- **Auto Focus and VR:** Although many F-mount lenses can be used with Auto Focus and Vibration Reduction (VR) thanks to the FTZ adapter, some older lenses might not be able to support these features when used with the Z50 II. Depending on the lens and adapter, performance will vary.
- **Lens Size and Weight:** When used with the Z50 II, the whole setup may seem a little more complicated since certain older F-mount lenses may be heavier and bulkier than contemporary Z-mount lenses.

Nevertheless, for photographers who have invested much in F-mount lenses and want to keep using them without having to buy new ones, the adapter is a viable choice.

Z-Mount Third-Party Lens Options

You would anticipate that there would be limited third-party lenses available because the Z-mount system is still relatively new. Nonetheless, a number of producers, such as Sigma, Tamron, and Viltrox, have quickly started creating Z-mount lenses, expanding the range. If you want to save money without sacrificing quality, these third-party lenses can be a great choice because they often offer great value for the money. It's also important to note that these lenses are frequently lighter and smaller than their F-mount counterparts, which complements the Z50 II's small form factor.

Future Developments in Lenses

Although Nikon's Z-mount technology is still in its infancy, the company has promised to expand its selection of Z-mount lenses. **We may anticipate more specialized lenses in the future, such as:**

- Super-telephoto lenses for sports and wildlife photography
- Wide-aperture primes for improved light capture and bokeh; and

↓ Specialty lenses like tilt-shift and fisheye to provide distinctive artistic effects.

This growing selection will guarantee that your lens options increase as your photographic skills advance, allowing you greater creative freedom.

Durability and Shutter Mechanism

The Nikon Z50 II's shutter mechanism is essential to its functionality, particularly with regard to longevity and performance in a range of shooting conditions. The Z50 II is a mirrorless camera that has a mechanical shutter for still images as well as an electronic shutter, providing photographers additional choices based on the kind of picture they want.

Knowing How the Shutter Works

DSLRs have a mirror that flips up to expose the sensor, but mirrorless cameras, like the Nikon Z50 II, do not. Rather, the digital viewfinder (also known as the rear LCD) of the camera shows the data being collected by the sensor in real time. In contrast, the shutter mechanism remains a crucial part of the camera since it regulates when the sensor is exposed to light, which enables the camera to capture an image.

Mechanical Shutter

In most circumstances, you'll wish to utilize the Z50 II's mechanical shutter. It physically opens and closes to expose the image sensor to light during the photo. This sort of shutter is typically more trustworthy in terms of giving a crisp picture, especially at high shutter speeds. The Z50 II's mechanical shutter can function at speeds of up to 1/4000 second. This allows you to freeze fast-moving objects while reducing motion blur.

Electronic Shutter

The electronic shutter of the Z50 II, on the other hand, is devoid of moving parts. Instead, the sensor is exposed to light electrically. The benefit of adopting an electronic shutter is that it enables for silent shooting, which is useful in scenarios where discretion is necessary, such as wildlife or concert photography. The Z50 II's electronic shutter can also attain unusually quick shutter speeds of up to 1/16000 second, making it suitable for highly bright conditions or high-speed photography. One downside of the electronic shutter is that it might cause visual distortions, particularly when capturing fast-moving objects under artificial illumination. This phenomenon, known as a rolling shutter, may sometimes cause bending or skewing of fast-moving objects, therefore employ the mechanical shutter if you wish to capture high-speed action shots.

Durability and Shutter Life

The lifetime of a camera's shutter mechanism is one of the most important factors in determining how long it will last. Over time, shutters may deteriorate, particularly in business settings. Like any camera, the Z50 II's shutter mechanism is reliable, but it's important to know how long it should last.

Rating for Shutter

The shutter rating of the Nikon Z50 II is approximately 200,000 actuations. This suggests that the shutter of the camera should endure about 200,000 pushes before exhibiting signs of wear and tear under normal operating conditions. This is adequate for the majority of users. You won't likely hit this number anytime soon unless you're shooting in high-volume situations (such as sports, news, or wedding photography). Similar to other mid-range mirrorless cameras in its class, the Z50 II's shutter endurance offers a robust and dependable lifespan for both professionals and enthusiasts. However, wear and tear may happen more quickly if you are shooting in extremely damp or dusty conditions or if you are shooting a lot of fast-paced action (which results in a lot of shutter actuations).

Durability of Electronic Shutter

The mechanical shutter wears out more rapidly than the electronic shutter since it has no moving components. As a result, you may use the electronic shutter for as long as you want without worrying about how long it will last. Since the electronic shutter won't be actuated as frequently, it's actually a great way for many photographers who do a lot of silent shooting to prolong the life of the mechanical shutter.

Shutter's Effect on Camera Performance

Practically speaking, the shutter mechanism of the Nikon Z50 II influences not only the ability to capture images but also the camera's performance when shooting continuously and recording videos.

Constant Shooting Performance

The Z50 II features a continuous shooting mode that enables a burst rate of up to 11 frames per second when taking action or sports photos. This is owing to the mechanical shutter, which can open and close swiftly enough to capture fast-moving objects. The electronic shutter may also be employed for quiet continuous shooting at up to 20 fps, which is perfect for instances when you wish to capture the event without attracting attention.

Video Performance

In video mode, the shutter is less significant than in stills as frame rate (rather than shutter speed) generally defines how video looks. However, the camera's ability to capture 4K UHD video and support features likes slow motion and time-lapse is reliant on the shutter system's seamless working to maintain constant exposure while recording. The shutter mechanism of the Z50 II will eliminate flicker and inconsistent exposure rates in your movies.

Preserving and Increasing the Life of the Shutter

You may do the following to extend the shutter's lifespan on your Nikon Z50 II:

- Use the electronic shutter for quiet photography if motion blur is not a problem. This will save wear on the mechanical shutter in addition to offering quiet operation.
- Use the auto power-off mode or switch off the camera to prevent unnecessary shutter actuations. By reducing the amount of actuations, this may extend the shutter mechanism's lifespan.
- **Keep your camera clean:** The shutter mechanism may get clogged with dust, dirt, and moisture, causing premature degradation. Maintain a clean, dry environment and clean your camera and lenses often.
- **Make use of the Z50 II as intended:** Deterioration may be accelerated by excessive usage, such as hostile conditions or constant burst firing. Take breaks in between intense photo sessions and use the camera as intended.

Noise Performance and ISO Range

A camera's ISO range and noise reduction capabilities are essential for taking excellent pictures, particularly in challenging lighting conditions. You can get the best results by knowing how the Nikon Z50 II handles exact details, fast-moving objects, and low-light photography.

ISO Range: What Is It?

The sensitivity of the image sensor of your camera to light is known as ISO. By increasing the sensitivity of the sensor, a higher ISO setting enables you to take pictures without the need of flash in low light conditions. But doing so comes at the price of picture noise, which might lower the caliber of your shots. With its exceptional ISO range, the Nikon Z50 II offers photographers a good balance between exposure and picture quality.

Normal ISO Range

For a camera of its kind, the Z50 II's native ISO range of 100 to 51,200 is quite broad. In order to take pictures in darker environments, you may start shooting at ISO 100 (low sensitivity) in full daylight and progressively raise the ISO as the light level drops.

- ISO 100 produces crisp images with little noise, making it suitable for broad daylight.
- The highest native ISO setting is 51,200, which permits low-light photography but results in increased noise (more on this later). This is the default setting for the majority of shooting situations, producing vivid colors and sharp details.

Increased ISO Range

With the Z50 II, you may raise the ISO range over the built-in restrictions for those situations when you really need to test your camera's sensitivity. For bright situations, the extended ISO range begins at ISO 50. For very low light conditions, it may reach ISO 204,800.

- ISO 50 is best suited for sunny days or situations when you want to use a wide aperture but still get a narrow depth of focus.
- ISO 204,800 is an extreme setting meant for very low light, such as indoor events with little illumination or shooting stars at night. Nevertheless, using this option will lead to a lot of noise and less clear images.

How Image Quality Is Affected by Noise

Noise is the main drawback of higher ISO settings. Noise may reduce the sharpness and clarity of your photos and cause graininess or color aberrations, especially in dark areas. Gaining the best performance from the Z50 II in a range of lighting conditions requires an understanding of how the camera responds to noise at various ISO settings.

Low ISO (between 100 and 400)

The Z50 II performs very well at low ISO settings, producing sharp, clean images with little noise. When shooting in bright environments, including during the day or in well-lit interior spaces, you should choose this range. There won't be much to no grain in your photos, and they will have sharp details and vibrant colors.

(ISO 800-1600) Mid ISO

In the mid-ISO range, the Z50 II continues to provide excellent results. Even while there is a little increase in noise, it is still quite manageable, especially for a low-cost mirrorless camera. For the majority of photographers, in situations like indoor portraiture or in the evening when natural light starts to fade, ISO 800 or ISO 1600 will be enough. At these settings, the noise level is usually so low that it is hardly noticeable on screen or in most printouts.

Elevated ISO (3200-6400)

Noise is more noticeable at higher ISO settings, while the Z50 II's integrated noise reduction technology greatly lessens it. For many photographers, the camera's ability to shoot high-quality images with controlled grain at ISO 3200 is enough. This range is perfect for basic indoor photography, events, and low-light portraits.

Extremely High ISO (12,800 or above)

As ISO is raised over ISO 6400, noise becomes more noticeable. Still, passable images at ISO 12,800 or ISO 25,600 may be taken thanks to the Z50 II's EXPEED 6 engine, which helps to minimize this with effective noise reduction. Depending on your needs, these photos may still work well in low light, especially for smaller prints or online use, even if you could notice a softening of tiny characteristics and a decrease in picture clarity.

ISO Extreme (ISO 51,200 or above)

Noise may increase significantly at ISO 51,200 and above, and the camera's noise reduction mechanism may smooth down images too much, erasing details. At this point, the picture quality of the Z50 II starts to drastically decline. Even while ISO 51,200 may still produce passable images, it would be wise to stay away from it for crucial photos that need a high level of detail and clarity. Due to severe noise levels and resolution loss, ISO 204,800 is not recommended for professional usage and should only be utilized in very specific conditions (such as very low light levels).

Performance and Noise Reduction

The Z50 II's capacity to manage high ISO noise is largely due to its EXPEED 6 CPU. The camera uses noise reduction algorithms to reduce noise while maintaining the sharpness and detail ratio when you increase the ISO. But sometimes, especially at high ISO levels, these methods might result in a loss of fine detail. Considering the Z50 II's price range,

Nikon performed an excellent job with noise reduction. It performs adequately for an entry-level mirrorless camera, but it won't be able to match with more expensive versions like the Z6 II or D850 for noise suppression at really high ISOs.

Useful Advice for Efficient ISO Utilization

- **Shoot at Lower ISOs When Possible:** Keep your ISO as low as you can, preferably between ISO 100 and 1600, to get the best picture quality. Photographs that are clearer and have better details and more vibrant colors will be the outcome of this.
- **Use Fast Lenses in Low-Light Conditions:** Try using f/1.8 or f/2.8 lenses if you need to raise the ISO since you're shooting in low light. You won't need to increase your ISO as much to get the proper exposure with these lenses since they allow more light to reach the sensor.
- **Make Use of the Camera's Noise Reduction Features:** The Z50 II includes adjustable built-in noise reduction features. You may change these settings to get a better balance between noise reduction and picture quality preservation if you're shooting at a higher ISO.
- **Shoot in RAW for Post-Processing Flexibility:** RAW gives you more post-processing choices for reducing noise and restoring lost information, especially if you end up using higher ISOs. Compared to JPEGs, RAW files include more information and provide you greater control over noise and exposure.
- **For quiet low-light photos, use the Electronic Shutter:** The Z50 II's electronic shutter eliminates the noise that comes with a mechanical shutter, making it perfect for taking quiet photos at higher ISOs. It works well for filming in serene locations such as theaters and churches.

Modes, Speed, and Points of the Autofocus System

The autofocus (AF) system of the Nikon Z50 II mirrorless camera is one of its noteworthy features. The capacity of the camera to focus rapidly and accurately may make or ruin an image, whether you're taking pictures of fast-moving objects, taking pictures in low light, or taking detailed portraits. This section will examine the autofocus technology of the Z50 II, including the possible AF settings, focusing speed, and number of focus points.

Where Are the Focus Points and How Many Are There?

Phase detection and contrast detection are both used in the hybrid focusing system of the Nikon Z50 II. Fast and reliable focusing performance is offered by this setup in a broad range of photography situations.

209 Points of Phase Detection

The Z50 II incorporates 209 phase-detection focusing points, which increase accuracy and speed. The camera has a broad focusing range because to the phase-detection AF points that are dispersed around the sensor. By detecting the difference in light between two regions of the image sensor, the phase-detection points are designed to focus quickly and precisely, especially while taking pictures of moving objects or in low light conditions.

- It helps track moving subjects by maintaining the lock on even while the subject is moving, and
- The phase-detection technology offers quick and accurate focusing for motionless subjects.

Detection of Contrast AF

The camera also uses contrast-detection autofocus, which is slower but more accurate than phase detection. Until the sharpest contrast is achieved, this technology examines the contrast of the picture and modifies focus. Even while contrast detection is slower than phase detection, it may still be useful for fine-tuning accuracy, particularly when taking pictures of stationary things at moderate speeds or in low light. These two mechanics work together to deliver smooth, quick, and accurate focusing in a range of illumination conditions.

What Is the Autofocus Speed?

For both novice and experienced photographers seeking a responsive system in a variety of situations, the Z50 II's auto focus mechanism is a great choice since it is surprisingly quick for its class.

Quick Acquisition of Focus

The Z50 II's phase-detection points allow for very quick autofocus. It is perfect for monitoring fast-moving things like athletes or animals since it can latch onto them in a split second. Additionally, subject tracking is fast, allowing you to capture action shots without lag. The Z50 II is among the quickest autofocus systems in its class, especially when compared to other entry- and mid-level mirrorless cameras, with a focus time of 0.08 seconds on average.

Performance in low light

Additionally, the Z50 II does well in low light conditions. It is particularly helpful for taking pictures in dimly lit areas, such indoor events, concerts, or nighttime street photography, since it can focus in light as low as -4 EV. The high sensitivity of the phase-detection sites and the overall sensor technology of the Z50 II make this possible. It suggests that even in low light conditions, the camera can maintain focus and capture clear images.

Changing Focus to Fit Your Shooting Style with Autofocus Modes

There are many autofocus settings on the Nikon Z50 II to suit various types of photography. These options allow you to customize the autofocus to your own requirements, whether you're shooting video, sports, or portraiture.

One-point AF

One of the most basic autofocus settings is the Single-Point AF mode. You may concentrate on a specific point or region out of the 209 possible AF sites. This is ideal for finely concentrating on a particular topic, such in portraiture when you need to draw attention to the individual's eyes or another significant feature.

 + Perfect for still photography with immobile subjects, this mode allows you to manipulate the camera's focus for sharp, detailed images.

Area AF Dynamic

You can specify a precise focus point using the Dynamic-Area AF mode, but the camera will use nearby focus points to maintain focus if the subject moves slightly away from the original AF point. This mode is ideal for capturing subjects that move suddenly while maintaining camera focus on the surrounding area. It is also ideal for objects that are moving but still need the camera to monitor and concentrate on them, as in sports or action photography.

Wide-area AF

Greater number of focus points is used across a larger portion of the frame in the Wide-Area AF mode. Because it enables the camera to focus across a wider region, this mode is perfect for photographing landscapes with dispersed objects or gatherings of people.

- Ideal for a variety of shooting situations, such as street photography and event coverage, the camera will choose the subject within the wider focus area, making it a great choice for quick, wide-field shots.

Auto-area AF

The best focus locations inside the frame are automatically chosen by the camera's Auto-Area AF setting. Using 209 AF points, it tracks subjects based on movement and scene structure. When you don't want to manually adjust the autofocus point and want the camera to focus everything for you, this option is quite helpful.

- When you don't have time to change focus points, such in street photography or spontaneous moment capture, use this option. When photographing fast-moving subjects in unpredictable situations, the camera will automatically choose the best focus zones.

Eye Detection AF

Eye Detection AF, one of the most remarkable features of the Z50 II, employs deep learning to recognize and focus on a subject's eye, even in dim light or when the face is partially turned. Because portrait photography requires sharp eyesight, this makes it ideal.

- Clear and precise portrait photographs are ensured by prioritizing the human eyes as the focus point. Eye Detection AF is very accurate, even when there are moving people or obstacles in the frame.

Tracking Subjects (AF)

The camera will track the moving subject automatically when you choose the Subject Tracking AF setting. When the subject is constantly moving across the frame, such as in sports or wildlife photography, this is quite helpful.

- This is ideal for recording fast-moving subjects without losing focus since, once locked onto the subject; the camera will maintain focus even if the subject moves across the frame or changes direction.

Autofocus for Videos

The focusing mechanism of the Z50 II is similarly outstanding when it comes to video filming. It may change focus while shooting since it supports continuous autofocus (AF-

C) in video mode. This helps maintain the subject's focus throughout the image, which is particularly helpful for photographing moving objects.

- With the aid of Eye AF, you can ensure that your subject's eyes remain focused even when they move throughout video.
- The camera's focus in the video is smooth and fast, with no noticeable hunting, making it perfect for vloggers and content creators who need quick and accurate focus transitions.

Continuous Shooting Speeds and Burst Mode

For photographers who need to capture fast-moving scenes or circumstances that need exact timing, burst mode—also referred to as continuous shooting—is an essential tool. Burst mode lets you snap a series of quick images, whether you're shooting sports, animals, or trying to capture the ideal candid moment. With its cutting-edge mirrorless design and exceptional burst speed, the Nikon Z50 II is an excellent option for action-packed photography.

How Quickly Can the Nikon Z50 II Take Pictures?

The Nikon Z50 II has exceptional continuous shooting speeds, particularly considering its compact size and affordable pricing. Photographers can record fast-paced action without missing a beat thanks to the Z50 II's strong EXPEED 6 image processor and 20.9 MP DX-format sensors, which are designed to handle high-speed shooting with ease.

With a mechanical shutter, you can shoot up to 11 frames per second

The Z50 II can shoot up to 11 frames per second using the mechanical shutter. For taking pictures of fast-moving objects like athletes, birds in flight, or racing cars on the track, this burst rate is perfect. The camera can capture a lot of pictures in a short amount of time at 11 frames per second, which improves your chances of getting the perfect action photo.

- **How It Aids:** Fast-paced action sequences benefit greatly from this speed as it enables quick filming without lag or frame-to-frame delays.
- **Buffer Capacity:** Before filling up, the camera may capture short bursts of images. About 30 JPEG or 10 RAW photos may be stored in the Z50 II's memory in a single, continuous burst. The camera then needs time to clear the buffer and be ready for the subsequent round of pictures. But for this kind of camera, this is rather generous.

Electronic shutter up to 30 frames per second (fps)

The Z50 II has an electronic shutter in addition to a mechanical shutter, allowing for even faster continuous shooting rates of up to 30 frames per second. Faster speeds and the elimination of any possible mechanical noise are achieved by the electronic shutter, which enables the camera to capture images without the shutter actually moving.

- **Ideal for Quiet Shooting:** Because of its silent operation, the electronic shutter is perfect for events or wildlife photography without disturbing the subject.
- **Electronic shutter limitations:** Even though the 30-fps speed is fantastic, using the electronic shutter might distort images that move quickly. Things or vertical lines bend strangely when fast motion is captured. In most photography situations, this is not an issue, but in situations involving very fast motion, like racing, the mechanical shutter could be the better option.

What Can Be Expected While Shooting Nonstop?

You typically want to take a lot of pictures fast while in burst mode, but the quality of those photographs and your ability to follow the subject are just as important as the speed. **Let's review some of the key components of the Nikon Z50 II's burst mode:**

Autofocus when shooting continuously

Because of its hybrid AF technology (phase-detection and contrast-detection), the Z50 II's autofocus system continues to function even while it is in burst mode. With tracking autofocus in particular, the camera will focus on targets in real-time while you shoot continuously, ensuring that the burst shots are sharp. However, be aware that tracking moving objects, especially at fast speeds, may sometimes cause slight focus variations if the subject moves erratically or the illumination changes quickly.

- The Z50 II can follow moving subjects in bursts while maintaining clarity and sharpness thanks to continuous subject auto (AF-C).
- Even in burst mode, the camera can follow and focus on your subject's eyes when Eye AF is turned on, producing crisp portraits.

Buffering and Shutter Lag

Even while the camera performs wonderfully at 11 frames per second (mechanical shutter) and 30 frames per second (electronic shutter), remember that continuous high-speed bursts of photography generate a substantial quantity of data. The buffer, which acts as a temporary storage space for photos while they are being captured, may fill up rapidly when shooting at high rates. There may be a little lag between bursts since the

Z50 II's buffer can only hold 30 JPEG images or 10 RAW files before having to be cleaned. The buffer may fill very fast while shooting in RAW format, which might cause some delay when the camera clears it. Conversely, shooting in JPEG will result in a longer burst without buffering. The camera will stop for a while to clear the buffer after the burst. Even though this delay isn't very lengthy, it's something to consider if you need to fire often in short succession.

Making Effective Use of Burst Mode

Photographers may get the best results by knowing when and how to use burst mode. When using the Nikon Z50 II in continuous mode, keep the following points in mind: Use it for subjects that move and for fast activity. Burst mode is very useful for photographing subjects that move quickly. **For instance:**

- **Sports photography:** Take pictures of athlete's mid-jump or at full speed.
- **Wildlife photography:** Take pictures of swiftly moving animals or birds in midair.
- **Street photography:** Take candid pictures without fear of missing anything.

Choose the Appropriate Shutter Mode

The electronic shutter might provide a notable speed boost, depending on the topic, especially if you want the camera to take quiet pictures. However, the mechanical shutter could be a better choice to get rid of the rolling shutter effect for situations with very rapid motion, like racing or a figure moving quickly across the frame.

Select an appropriate AF mode

AF-C (Continuous Autofocus), which enables the camera to continuously adjust focus as you shoot, is the best setting for continuous photography. To assist the camera in effectively following targets, choose an appropriate AF area setting, such as Wide Area AF or Dynamic Area AF.

Check the file format and buffer

Determine how many photos you can obtain before the buffer fills up before heading out to shoot in burst mode. Because the camera can process more JPEG files before slowing down, you may want to switch to JPEG if you're taking large bursts of photographs quickly. Depending on the shooting conditions, you may want to switch to a different file format since RAW files take up a lot more space.

CHAPTER THREE
LEARNING TO USE THE NIKON Z50 II FOR PHOTOGRAPHY

Fundamental Ideas in Photography

ISO, shutter speed, and aperture

Being a skilled photographer requires knowing the basic ideas behind ISO, shutter speed, and aperture. Together, these three elements—sometimes referred to as the exposure triangle—control the exposure and caliber of your photos. Each of them has a distinct function, and knowing how they work together enables you to make imaginative and effective changes to your camera settings.

Aperture: The Camera's Eye

The amount of light that enters the camera is controlled by the lens's aperture. Think of it as the pupil of an eye that expands or contracts in response to the amount of light needed. **Aperture, measured in f-stops (e.g., f/2.8, f/5.6, f/11), affects your picture in two ways:**

  - A wide aperture (e.g., f/2.8) narrows the depth of field, softening the background while intensifying the subject in focus. This is perfect for portraiture, when you want the person to stand out. A small aperture (f/16) creates a deep depth of field, keeping both the foreground and background in focus. This is especially useful for landscape photography, which demands high-quality detail across the frame.
  - It is ideal for low light conditions because of its wide aperture (small f-number), which lets in more light. When you want to more precisely manage the exposure or in bright environments, a small aperture (large f-number) is helpful since it lets in less light.

Useful advice

  - To blur the background and draw attention to the subject in portraiture, use a wide aperture (f/2.8 to f/5.6).
  - Use a modest aperture (f/11 to f/16) for landscape photography to get strong focus from the background to the foreground.

Using Shutter Speed to Record Motion

The length of time the camera's shutter stays open to let light into the sensor is known as the shutter speed. It may be stated in whole seconds (e.g., one second, five seconds) or fractions of a second (e.g., 1/500, 1/1000).

- Use a fast shutter speed (e.g., 1/1000 or 1/500) to freeze subjects that move quickly. For instance, taking pictures of a vehicle speeding by, a bird in flight, or an athlete moving quickly. It keeps your topic sharp and clear while removing motion blur.
- By letting more light reach the sensor, lower shutter rates (such as 1/30 or 1/2 second) may provide the impression that a picture is moving. For instance, while photographing a waterfall or a busy street, slow shutter speeds might highlight the movement of people and cars or turn water into a smooth blur. Lower shutter speeds may require the use of a tripod to prevent camera shaking and maintain picture stability.

Useful advice

- To freeze motion in action shots, such as those of sports, use a fast shutter speed.
- To catch motion, such flowing water, or to produce light trails at night, use a slow shutter speed.

ISO: Light Sensitivity

The sensitivity of your camera's sensor to light is known as ISO. The sensitivity of the sensor increases with the ISO level, enabling you to take pictures in low light conditions. However, increasing ISO, especially at higher settings, might result in noise (graininess) in your picture.

- For brighter conditions or longer tripod exposures, choose a low ISO (such as ISO 100 or ISO 200). A low ISO maintains a clear, noise-free picture.
- High ISO (such as ISO 1600 or ISO 3200): This improves light sensitivity and enables flash-free photography in low light. The trade-off, however, is more noise. You can see a grainy texture in the image's midtones or shadows if you set the ISO too high.

Useful advice

- Use a tripod for longer exposures or a low ISO (100–400) when taking pictures outside in strong light.

- Use a higher ISO (800–1600) while shooting inside or at night, but don't go overboard to minimize noise.

The interactivity of the Exposure Triangle

The shutter speed, ISO, and aperture are all closely related to one another. Sometimes adjustments to one setting need adjustments to the others in order to maintain ideal exposure.
- As the aperture (f-number) increases, less light reaches the sensor, necessitating a higher ISO or slower shutter speed to make up for it.
- Reduce the aperture (f-number) to let in more light in order to avoid overexposure. This enables you to adjust the ISO or shutter speed as necessary.
- Increase the ISO or widen the aperture (use a lower f-number) to make sure enough light reaches the sensor in order to capture rapid action with a fast shutter time.

Bringing Everything Together

Let's say you're taking a sunset shot of a soccer match:
- Use a high shutter speed (such as 1/1000) for freezing action.
- Use a wide aperture (such as f/2.8 or f/4) to keep the subject sharp and isolated from the background.
- Consider raising the ISO to 800 or 1600 to account for diminishing light after sunset.

Fundamental Photography Ideas for the Nikon Z50 II: ISO, shutter speed, and aperture

Aperture Regulates Depth of Field and Light

To get the perfect depth of focus for your photo, you can easily adjust the Z50 II's aperture using the control dials. More light may enter the camera with a bigger aperture (f/1.8, for example), which is helpful for creating shallow depth of focus and in low light conditions. Especially in portraiture, this effect is perfect for setting a figure out from the background. Conversely, using a smaller aperture (f/8, for example) produces a greater depth of focus and maintains sharpness across the frame, which is advantageous for landscape photography. With the Z50 II, you may increase the aperture while shooting in low light, giving you more flexibility without significantly raising the ISO. You can also quickly adjust aperture settings using the touchscreen while shooting in Live View mode, which makes it easier to see how changes will impact exposure in real time.

Stopping or Creating Motion with Shutter Speed

The shutter speed of the camera controls how long the shutter stays open to let light into the sensor. With shutter speeds ranging from 1/4000 of a second to 30 seconds, the Z50 II offers a wide range of possibilities for capturing different types of movement. Use a fast shutter speed (such as 1/1000) for subjects that move quickly, such as sports or animals, to minimize motion blur and freeze the action. Alternatively, a slower shutter speed (e.g., 1/30 or 2 seconds) can work well if you want to create motion blur, such when you're photographing the water's flow or light trails at night. In-body image stabilization (IBIS) of the Z50 II also helps to reduce camera shaking, especially when taking handheld pictures with shorter shutter rates. When photographing in low light or around sunset, this feature is quite helpful.

ISO: modifying light sensitivity

The sensitivity of the camera sensor to light is affected by the ISO setting. With a range of ISO settings that let you adjust the sensitivity without introducing too much noise, the Z50 II performs very well in low light conditions. The cleanest, clearest picture is produced when the ISO is kept low (e.g., ISO 100) under bright light. Increasing the ISO (for instance, ISO 1600 or ISO 3200) allows the camera to capture more light while shooting in low light, but keep in mind that a higher ISO might introduce noise. You may raise the ISO as needed without sacrificing picture quality since the Z50 II performs very well at higher ISOs. Additionally, you may use the Z50 II Auto's Auto ISO mode, which allows you to concentrate on composition while the camera automatically adjusts the ISO depending on the illumination.

White Metering and Balance

Regardless of the lighting, white balancing is the process of altering the colors in your photos so that white objects seem really white without any artificial color tints. Different light sources, including sunlight, fluorescent lights, or tungsten bulbs, produce different color temperatures. If you don't adjust them correctly, your photos may seem too warm (yellow/orange) or too cold (blue).

How the Nikon Z50 II White Balance Operates

Depending on the illumination, the Z50 II has a variety of white balance settings to assist you get the right color tone:

- **Auto White Balance (AWB):** This option adjusts the white balance for you based on lighting conditions. Although AWB works well in typical situations, it may not be able to handle harsh illumination or situations that call for human adjustment.
- **Presets:** For typical light sources, the camera features presets like:
  - **Daylight:** For photographs taken outside in the sun.
  - **Tungsten:** For photos taken inside using incandescent lights.
  - For fluorescent lights, use fluorescent.
  - **Cloudy:** For cloudy settings, when a somewhat warmer tone is needed.
- **Custom White Balance:** You may manually alter the white balance to ensure flawless color accuracy or if you're shooting in unusual settings. This involves calibrating the white balance rate by taking a picture of a white or gray card in the ambient light.
- **Kelvin Temperature:** By inputting a Kelvin value (K), the Z50 II allows you to manually adjust the white balance. This is particularly beneficial for photographers who want absolute control over their color temperature. For instance, tungsten lights are around 3000K, but daylight typically varies from 5200K to 6000K.

Real-world Tip: Auto White Balance may not always provide the best results in mixed illumination, such as interior lighting with daylight coming in via a window. To ensure that the colors seem accurate in these situations, adjust the Kelvin value manually or use Custom White Balance.

Metering: Controlling Exposure for Precise Photographs

A camera uses metering to determine the right exposure settings (aperture, shutter speed, and ISO) by tracking the amount of light in a scene. To assist ensure that your photos are neither too dark (underexposed) nor too bright (overexposed), the Z50 II has multi-mode metering.

Settings for the Nikon Z50 II's Metering

- The most common and default metering method is matrix metering. To choose the best exposure, it evaluates the whole scene, including color, contrast, and brightness. For the majority of general photography situations, including street, portrait, and landscape photography, the Z50 II uses matrix metering to balance light across the picture.
- **Center-Weighted Metering:** This setting takes into consideration the surrounding region while highlighting the light in the center of the frame. When taking pictures of a person against a brighter backdrop, for example, and you

want the exposure to concentrate more on the subject in the middle of the frame, this is a great alternative.

- **Spot Metering:** This technique based the exposure on the detection of light in a very small region of the frame, usually the center or the area you concentrate on. This is useful in situations when you wish to expose a particular subject or portion of the image that is much brighter or darker than the rest of the image, as in high contrast situations (a figure in the shade with a beautiful sky behind them, for example).
- **Partial Metering:** This mode maintains focus on the central topic while detecting light from a wider range than spot metering. It provides adaptability in a range of lighting conditions and lies in the middle between center-weighted and spot metering.

Real-world Tip: By focusing on the subject's face or other important area to make sure they're well-lit, Spot Metering may assist you in exposing your shot effectively when you're shooting in a backlit situation with a darker subject than the background.

White Balance and Metering Together: Useful Applications

Together, white balance and metering provide the best picture possible. For instance, choosing the right white balance (like the Tungsten preset) while shooting inside in artificial lighting will ensure that the colors seem realistic, but utilizing the right metering mode (like Center-Weighted for portraiture) will assure that the exposure is superb.

- To guarantee crisp, well-lit photos while shooting in low light, choose a higher ISO and Auto White Balance. If your photos are too warm, you may manually alter the white balance using the Kelvin scale or change it to fluorescent.
- Use Auto White Balance for daytime photography outdoors. Use Spot Metering to expose a particular region of the picture or Matrix Metering to balance the light across the frame if you need to regulate exposure for highlights and shadows.
- **Creative Impacts:** Image mood may be affected by metering and white balance changes. For instance, you may use Spot Metering to highlight a subject against a bright backdrop or Tungsten White Balance to get a warm, golden color even in daylight.

Modes of shooting

You can customize how your camera responds to exposure, aperture, shutter speed, and other factors with the Nikon Z50 II's several shooting modes. From complete beginners to experienced photographers, these settings appeal to a broad spectrum of ability levels. Knowing how each mode works will enable you to choose the best one for your shooting circumstances, giving you the flexibility to try different things and get the effects that you want. We'll examine each of the Z50 II's main shooting modes below, along with when and how to use them.

Putting the Camera in Charge in Auto Mode

The Z50 II has complete control over all exposure parameters, including ISO, shutter speed, and aperture, while in Auto Mode. For beginners or those who just want to point and shoot without worrying about settings, this mode is designed. The camera automatically adjusts all settings based on the lighting conditions of the scene. When you don't have time to change settings or aren't sure which settings are best for a certain situation, use Auto Mode. It's perfect for quick pictures, informal photos, or when you're learning how to use a camera and want to concentrate on composition.

- **Advantages:** The primary benefit of Auto Mode is its ease of use. Simply press the shutter, and the camera will take care of the rest; you don't need to worry about technical aspects like white balance or the exposure triangle. Based on scene analysis, the Z50 II uses its built-in sensor and processing power to provide a balanced exposure.
- **Constraints:** This mode lacks creative control, despite its usefulness. For instance, you won't be able to regulate the motion blur or choose a certain depth of focus. Additionally, the ISO is set by the camera, which may raise it in low light to produce fuzzy images.

Automated Exposure with Flexibility in Programmed Auto (P)

The camera can still regulate exposure settings in Programmed Auto (P) mode, which is an improvement above Auto Mode. The Z50 II automatically selects the shutter speed and aperture for a balanced exposure while in P Mode, but you can also adjust other settings like ISO and white balance. Additionally, you may adjust the shutter speed or aperture while maintaining the same exposure value (EV). For quick results with manual control over exposure correction and ISO, use P Mode. For beginners who want to try with artistic exposure tweaks without committing to full manual control, it's also helpful.

- **Advantages:** Although Auto setting is still mostly automated, this setting gives you more control. The aperture/shutter speed combination, exposure correction, and ISO may all be changed. To preserve exposure, the Z50 II will automatically adjust the other settings.
- **Constraints:** Despite its adaptability, P Mode still lacks the full control of more advanced modes like as Manual Mode, Shutter Priority, and Aperture Priority. You cannot completely lock your shutter speed or aperture if you want to create a very accurate artistic effect.

Priority of Shutter (S): Blurred Motion or Freezing

In Shutter Priority (S) mode, the camera automatically adjusts the aperture to maintain the correct exposure, but you may still manage the shutter speed. This mode works well in circumstances when precise motion control is necessary. You may create motion blur with a slow shutter speed or freeze fast-moving objects with a quick shutter speed. For taking action photos of animals, sports, and other moving objects, S Mode is perfect. This mode is helpful for blurring moving objects (like a vehicle or water) to give the appearance of motion or freezing a moving image (like a bird in flight).

- **Advantages:** You have complete control over your motions in this mode. Depending on how fast or slow the action is in the scene, you may change the shutter speed to get the effect you want. To ensure proper exposure, the camera will automatically change the aperture to match.
- **Constraints:** Since the camera will choose the aperture, S Mode does not provide direct control over depth of field, even though it may freeze or blur motion. The camera could be compelled to utilize a high ISO, which might introduce noise, or a very wide aperture, which would not produce the appropriate depth of focus, in low light.

Priority of Aperture (A): Regulating Depth of Field

In order to guarantee correct exposure, the camera automatically adjusts the shutter speed while you select the aperture in Aperture Priority (A) mode. When you want to adjust the depth of field—the portion of your picture that is in focus from foreground to background—this setting is perfect. Controlling the depth of field in photos, such as in landscapes with crisp focus or portraits with a blurred backdrop, is made easier using aperture priority.

- **Advantages:** Precise focus on the scene is made possible by full aperture control. To guarantee ideal exposure, the camera automatically adjusts the shutter speed. It's a great option for preserving sharp vistas and adjusting artistic elements like bokeh.
- **Constraints**: The camera may utilize a high ISO or a fast shutter speed in low light, which might lead to noisy images or overexposed highlights. Furthermore, the camera may still choose a quick shutter speed that is inappropriate for your artistic goals even if you select a very wide aperture in a bright setting.

Manual (M): Total Authority over Exposure

You may get the ideal exposure by using Manual Mode (M), which gives you total control over the shutter speed and aperture. If the exposure is balanced, underexposed, or overexposed, the Z50 II will show a metering scale on the LCD or in the viewfinder. The ideal choice for seasoned photographers who want complete control over exposure settings is Manual Mode. It's ideal for taking pictures in challenging or imaginative lighting conditions, such at sunrise or sunset, or when you want to create a certain effect, like long exposures or purposeful under/overexposure.

- **Advantages:** Complete command over the exposure triangle, which includes ISO, shutter speed, and aperture. This is particularly crucial when attempting to create a particular artistic effect or while filming in difficult lighting conditions.
- **Constraints:** Experience and an understanding of the interplay between settings are necessary since you have control over every aspect of exposure. The Z50 II's exposure meter may assist you decide whether to take overexposed or underexposed photos if you're not sure.

Modes of Autofocus

The robust autofocus (AF) system of the Nikon Z50 II is designed to be adaptable in a range of shooting scenarios. The camera features a variety of autofocus settings to suit different needs, whether you're monitoring fast-moving action or focusing on a stationary subject.

One-point AF

This is one of the most precise focusing settings on the market. You may manually choose a precise focus point within the frame using Single-Point AF. After then, the camera only focuses on that spot. When you want to carefully control where the camera focuses, this mode is ideal for taking still photos, including macros or portraits. It offers a clear, precise focus on the subject's targeted region, like a person's eye in a photograph. Because you have to change the focus point every time the topic moves, it is less effective with moving subjects. When used with controlled participants, this technique yields extremely reliable results, but it requires more time and care.

Area AF Dynamic

Using Dynamic-Area AF gives us more flexibility when working with moving objects. The camera tracks the topic as it moves by using surrounding points, but you still choose the focus point. This facilitates the tracking of objects that may not stay perfectly still at a single focal point, such animals moving or sportsmen running. Dynamic-Area AF has the benefit of being able to respond to minute variations in the subject's position without becoming distracted. It may not provide the same pinpoint accuracy as Single-Point AF, but it is better at tracking moving objects. When subjects move erratically or suddenly change direction, it may have trouble tracking them since the camera may not always choose the ideal focus point.

Auto-area AF

By automatically selecting focus points depending on the situation, the Auto-Area AF mode takes full control of the focus for you. It's particularly useful in situations when you don't have time or want to manually adjust settings, such in fast-paced photography or when the subject moves suddenly. The camera quickly examines the surroundings to decide where to focus, even if your subject moves around the frame. For beginners or for shooting in dynamic environments, like street photography or catching fleeting moments, this mode is perfect. The drawback is that you have less artistic control over the focal point. It could choose the wrong focus locations if the frame has a lot of subjects.

Face tracking and eye detection

Eye-Detection AF is revolutionary when it comes to portrait photography. By automatically identifying and focusing on the subject's eye, this cutting-edge technology makes sure that the most important aspect of the picture is sharply focused. Combining this technology with Face Tracking allows the Z50 II to highlight human face images, which is particularly helpful for group and portrait photography as well as when the subject is moving. Eye-Detection AF and Face Tracking work together to keep the face firmly focused no matter how the subject moves or how complex the background is. It is quite effective, albeit it could have trouble with non-human figures or backdrops that are busy and have a lot of faces. The camera may sometimes lock onto the incorrect face if there are a lot of faces visible.

Choosing the Proper AF Mode

To suit a range of shooting techniques, the Z50 II has many focusing settings. While Dynamic-Area AF and Auto-Area AF aid in tracking moving objects, Single-Point AF offers precise control for stationary situations. For portraiture, Eye-Detection and Face Tracking are quite helpful since they guarantee that the most important element of the frame is always in focus. By knowing the advantages and disadvantages of each setting, you may choose the one that best suits the scene and subject you're shooting. These settings provide you the means to get crisp, accurate focus in a range of situations, regardless of your level of expertise as a photographer.

Using the Creative and Scene Modes

Scene Modes: Smart Configurations for Particular Circumstances

The Z50 II has preset settings called Scene Modes that automatically adjust the camera's properties according to the scene you're photographing. When quick adjustments are needed or you're still learning how to use the camera manually, these modes remove the uncertainty associated with choosing the right settings.

- When taking portrait photos, the camera's focus and exposure are improved by using the Portrait Mode preset. It is ideal for close-up shots of people because it produces a somewhat blurred background (shallow depth of field) while maintaining the subject's face in sharp focus. Additionally, the camera may enhance skin tones to provide a more visually pleasing picture.
- For wide-angle panoramas or natural sceneries, use Landscape Mode to concentrate both the foreground and background. Colors are regularly increased to provide a richer, more vibrant image, and the camera adapts to accentuate sharp details in the surrounding area.
- Sports mode is perfect for taking pictures of things that move quickly. The camera's settings are changed to improve freeze motion and shutter speed, producing crisp, clear images of athletes, animals, or anything else moving quickly.
- For taking pictures of people in low light, the Night Portrait Mode is ideal. In order to get a balanced image, it uses a slower shutter speed and flash to properly expose the subject while letting some background ambient light show through.
- The Close-Up (Macro) Mode allows the camera to focus closer, producing sharp details even at close range, making it ideal for photographing little objects like flowers or insects.

If you're new to photography or want to take a fast, stunning picture without changing every setting, these Scene Modes may be useful. You don't have to manually change the exposure, shutter speed, or aperture since the camera adapts to each situation.

Artistic Effects for Your Photographs: Creative Modes

By adding unique visual effects to your photos, the Z50 II's Creative Modes are designed to offer you more creative control and versatility. These settings provide distinctive styles that may drastically alter the mood of your photos in addition to adjusting the exposure and focus.

An outline of a few of these modes is provided below:

- To draw attention to a topic, use Selective Color, which converts a picture to black and white while preserving the full richness of a particular color. This striking effect is often used to draw attention to a single element in the picture, such a red outfit against a sea of greys.
- The Toy Camera Effect makes pictures seem vignette-like and faded, like toy or plastic lens cameras. It may provide a fun, vintage feel to your photos.
- Pop produces more vibrant colors by enhancing picture contrast and saturation. It's a great substitute for taking more striking or eye-catching pictures.
- High-key and low-key effects alter exposure to produce images with a lot of contrast. While Low-Key creates a darker, moodier appearance with sharper shadows, High-Key creates a bright, overexposed picture with soft shadows.
- In low light conditions, the Night Vision option increases brightness, producing an odd, brilliant appearance that turns dreary surroundings into surreal settings.

Using Picture Controls

Picture Controls on the Nikon Z50 II provide photographers complete control over the look and feel of their images. These are the default settings that determine how your photographs' colors, contrast, sharpness, and general tone appear. You may adjust the look of your photos to fit your own style or the mood you want to create by knowing how to use these tools. Picture controls are very helpful since they let you edit your photos in-camera instead of using post-processing software, which saves time and work while still resulting in a polished image. Each of the Picture Control settings on the Z50 II is designed to suit a different shooting situation or creative goal.

Image Controls by Default: Common Styles for Various Circumstances

The Nikon Z50 II has a number of preset Picture Control settings that are specific to different types of photos when you first use it. **These are easily accessible and may be selected right away from the menu on the camera.**

- **Standard:** This is the default configuration, intended for daily usage. From landscapes to portraits, it offers a well-balanced appearance with organic contrast and hues, making it appropriate for a broad range of topics. It's the greatest option if you want a simple, realistic portrayal free of too dramatic hues or contrast.
- **Neutral:** This Picture Control option produces a flatter picture by lowering saturation and contrast. It's ideal for post-processing because it provides a more

flexible starting point for editing by preserving more information in the highlights and shadows. Neutral is a fantastic option if you want to make a lot of modifications in programs like Lightroom or Photoshop.

- **Vibrant:** As the name implies, this setting intensifies color saturation, giving your images vivid, striking hues. For photos where you want the colors to pop, like street photography, landscapes, or any other scenario with plenty of color, Vivid is ideal. It may sometimes make skin tones seem odd in portraiture, so use it sparingly.
- **Monochrome:** This option records black and white pictures and lets you modify the sharpness and contrast to create a grayscale appearance. Monochrome is the best option if you want to achieve a timeless, classic style while taking street or portrait photos. Additionally, you may use filters to create even more imaginative effects, such as contrast-enhancing red or yellow filters.
- **Portrait:** This setting is perfect for taking portraits since it is adjusted for skin tones. It improves color accuracy and somewhat lessens overall contrast, making your subject's skin seem smooth and natural. This is ideal for taking pictures of people's faces without making them seem harsh or overexposed.
- **Landscape:** This Picture Control setting enhances the contrast and saturation of the colors, particularly in the blues and greens, to make the sky and vegetation more prominent in landscape or nature photos. Additionally, it highlights subtle details in textures, which makes it ideal for scenic or dramatic panoramas.

Adapting Picture Controls to Your Requirements

Although the Nikon Z50 II's built-in Picture Controls are useful in many situations, you may also adjust these settings to suit your own preferences or the unique look you're going for. You have even more creative control over how the camera processes the picture by adjusting individual parameters like Sharpness, Contrast, Brightness, Saturation, and Hue.

For instance:

- You may improve landscape photos by adjusting contrast and sharpness in Landscape mode.
- You may adjust the Saturation and Sharpness in Portrait mode to give your subject a gentle, organic appearance if you're taking photographs and want to capture pleasing skin tones.
- You may experiment with various filter effects (such red or green filters) to alter the brightness of particular colors in a monochrome picture. This might highlight textures in your subject or enhance the sky, giving certain areas of your shot more drama or depth.

Getting to and Changing the Picture Controls

Use these procedures to access and modify the Z50 II's Picture Controls:

- Press the button for picture control.
- **Choose Your Picture Control:** A list of the available settings (Standard, Vivid, Neutral, etc.) will appear. Select the one that best suits your requirements.
- **Customize (Optional):** You may change a Picture Control's settings after choosing one. Sharpness, Contrast, Saturation, and more settings are available. To customize any of these attributes to your liking, use the multi-selector.
- **Save and Apply:** The camera will apply your settings to the current photo when you save them once you're happy with them.

CHAPTER FOUR
EXAMINING THE MENUS OF THE NIKON Z50 II

The menus on the Nikon Z50 II are one of the main methods to customize the camera, which is intended to provide photographers a great deal of control over the quality of their images. You may adjust exposure, focusing, picture quality, and even the way you record videos using these options. If you learn to use these options, you can customize the camera to do precisely what you want it to, regardless of your level of experience. We will examine each of the Nikon Z50 II's menus and describe their functions in this chapter. From basic settings like ISO and white balance to more intricate settings that might help you get the best results for your photographic style, we'll cover it all. You will know more about how to configure your camera and customize it to your personal shooting preferences at the conclusion of this chapter.

The Menu for Setup

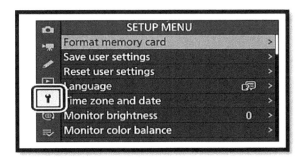

Memory Card Format

You may configure or reset your memory card using this option. To start the formatting process, click "Yes" after choosing the memory card slot. Without specialized recovery software, restoring lost files after formatting is almost impossible since it removes all data on the card and establishes a new file system. It resets the file allocation table (FAT or exFAT), which tells your computer and camera where to find your pictures. In essence, formatting gives the card a fresh look.

Configuration language

You may choose the language for the settings and menus on your camera here. Depending on where the camera was bought, several languages could be accessible.

Date and Time Zone

This option modifies the internal time and date of the camera.
Among the options are:
+ **Time Zone:** Use the little map on the screen to choose your location. If you travel, don't forget to update this so that your images are properly time-stamped.
+ **Date and Time:** Fill in the relevant fields with the year, month, day, hour, minute, and second.
+ Select a date format such as D/M/Y (day/month/year), M/D/Y (month/day/year), or Y/M/D (year/month/day).
+ **Daylight Saving Time:** Adjust this parameter to reflect changes in daylight saving time. Remember that the start date of daylight saving time changes every year, so you may need to check and modify this from time to time.

About monitor Brightness

The brightness of your camera's display may be changed using this option.
+ The brightness may only be adjusted while the display is in use. The brightness adjustment is turned off while the viewfinder is in use.
+ Increasing brightness may cause your battery to deplete more quickly.
+ Increasing brightness may affect the appearance of highlights, decreasing their clarity, if [HLG] mode is used for either shooting or playback.

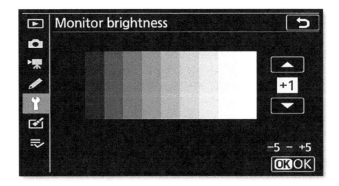

Keep an eye on the color balance

Your monitor's color tone may be adjusted to your liking.

- Only when the display is turned on does this option function. If you are using the viewfinder, it will not work.
- The two axes of color adjustment are blue/amber and green/magenta.
- These changes solely impact the shooting display, playback, and menus that you see on the monitor. The colors of your images or videos remain unchanged.

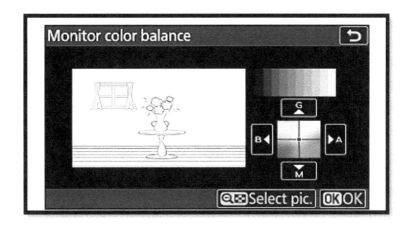

To modify:

- Make use of the reference image that is on the screen. A thumbnail of the most recent picture will appear in the upper-left corner of the screen.
- The last picture you looked at will show up if you're in playback mode. By clicking the Zoom Out button and looking through the thumbnails on your memory card, you may also choose a different picture.
- Adjust the color balance by using the directional controls.
- Click the icon to choose a different image. To choose the appropriate image as the reference image, highlight it and hit J.

Brightness of the Viewfinder

Only when the viewfinder is the active display is it possible to change the brightness. If the monitor is on or the monitor mode is set to monitor only, you won't be able to change it. The "Auto" brightness option on the electronic viewfinder automatically adjusts the brightness according to the lighting conditions in the room. However, there is also a manual brightness adjustment option for the display. When utilizing Manual mode, you may change the screen's brightness within a range of +/- 5 to make it darker or brighter. From the perspective of grayscale patches, this is useful. To adjust the brightness, use the multi-selector's up and down buttons. Press OK to preserve the change and go back to the menu if you're happy.

- **Important Tip:** The battery will deplete more quickly at higher brightness settings.
- You can see variations in tone display both during picture taking and playback if you adjust the Viewfinder Brightness in the configuration menu while using the HLG Tone Mode (High Dynamic Range). Increasing brightness may degrade picture quality, particularly in highlights and other bright regions.

Color Balance in the Viewfinder

You have the ability to adjust the viewfinder's color balance to your liking. Only when the viewfinder is being utilized as the primary display can this setting be altered. When the monitor is turned on or the Monitor Only mode is chosen, it is not accessible. The procedure for making adjustments is similar to that for Monitor Color Balance.

Size of Viewfinder Display (Photo Lv)

There are two sizes available for the viewfinder display: Standard and Small. In certain photography situations, it might be useful to choose Small since it makes the whole subject more visible.

Brightness of REC lamps

During time-lapse or video recordings, the REC lamp illuminates, and its brightness may be changed to your preference. There is an option to completely disable it, and the brightness settings range from 3 (brightest) to 1 (dimmest).
Choices:

- **Video Recording:** The brightness of the REC light is adjusted for video recording. While recording, the REC bulb will illuminate if any other option is selected than off.
- **Recording Time-Lapse recordings:** This modifies the brightness of the REC light especially for time-lapse recordings. During time-lapse recording, the REC bulb will flash twice rapidly at regular intervals if the battery is low.

Options for AF Fine-Tuning

You may adjust the focus for your current lens using these settings. Make use of this function only when required and at a focus distance that you often use. The adjustment may not be as effective at greater distances if you fine-tune at a low focus distance.

Important Configurations

- **AF Fine Tune (On/Off):** When you turn this on, the camera will use your personalized fine-tuning settings to focus more accurately.
- **Adjust and save Lens:** You have the option to save the fine-tuning parameters for certain lenses.
  - ➤ The focal point is moved farther away from the lens by positive values (+1 to +20).
  - ➤ The focus point is brought closer to the lens by negative values (-1 to -20).
  - ➤ **Dual Value Display:** For convenient comparison, the camera displays both the past and current fine-tuning values.
  - ➤ **Multiple Lenses:** Up to 40 lenses fine-tuning settings may be stored on the Nikon Z50 II.
  - ➤ **Existing Values:** You may change or remove any stored values for the lens.

The default value

For all lenses that haven't been altered yet, you may change the fine-tuning option by default. If many lenses have trouble focusing on the subject, either in front of or beyond the desired focal point, this might be helpful. Use caution while use this function, however, since it can affect the camera's CPU lens performance.

List of Values Saved

It allows you to see and modify all of your stored fine-tuning settings. When you utilize the [Fine-Tune and Save Lens] feature, the camera shows the settings that were stored. **Use this tool by doing the following:**

- **Highlight and Select:** The [Choose Lens Number] box will appear once you choose a lens from the list and hit 2.
- **Lens Identifier:** For Z-mount and certain F-mount lenses, you have the option of manually entering the lens identifier or allowing the camera to automatically enter the serial number.

Select the Current Lens's Value

You may quickly choose the appropriate fine-tuning option from the list if you have stored several for the same kind of lens. This function guarantees that every lens is properly set up for your unique shooting needs and makes setting adjustments easy.

Non-CPU Lens Information

Keep track of data for lenses that need an extra mount adapter because they lack a built-in CPU. By adjusting the focal length and maximum aperture of non-CPU lenses, you may still use some camera capabilities, such as vibration reduction, that are exclusive to CPU lenses.

+ **Lens Number:** Giving each lens a number enables the camera to precisely modify its settings, which is particularly useful when utilizing many lenses.
+ **Length of Focus (mm):** Enter the focal length of the lens. This information is important since it influences the application of the fine-tuning adjustments. Make sure the focal length is specified in millimeters (mm) for accurate calibration.
+ **Maximum Aperture:** Adjust the maximum aperture of the lens. The biggest aperture of the lens, allowing the most light to enter, is represented by the lowest f-number. This option is crucial for managing the depth of field and sharpness of the picture. Will selecting the appropriate maximum aperture enable more precise focus adjustments?

Units of Distance

When focusing manually, this displays the distance between the subject and the camera. The distance units may be changed to either feet or meters.

+ Remember that depending on the lens being used, the distance shown is just an estimate and could not be entirely correct.

Preserve the Focus Position

If [ON] is chosen, the camera will remember its most recent focus setting even after it has been switched off and will revert to it upon turning it back on. The camera could take longer to set up as a result, however.

+ The focus may be different when the camera is switched back on than when it was out of commission. Variations in temperature zoom adjustments, or other motions while the camera is off may all cause this.
+ It's also crucial to remember that even if [OFF] is chosen, the emphasis could go back to its original location. Depending on the camera and lens being utilized, this behavior may change.

PZ Lenses: Save Zoom Position

The camera will remember the zoom position when it is switched off and return to that zoom setting when it is powered back on if [ON] is chosen and a power zoom (PZ) lens is connected.

Dust off the image reference photo

You must first put the camera in picture mode and choose it in order to collect reference data for picture Dust-Off.

Obtaining Reference Information for Dust-Off Images

+ **Select a starting option:**
  - ➤ To instantly open the [Image Dust Off ref photo] box, choose [Start] and hit the "OK" button.

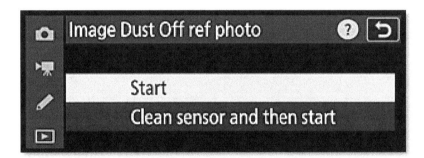

  - ➤ Prior to beginning, choose "Clean sensor and then start" and hit "OK" to clean the image sensor. The [Image Dust Off ref photo] window will show up when the sensor has been cleaned.
  - ➤ To depart without learning more about Image Dust Off, use the MENU button.

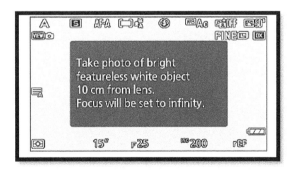

- **Present the topic:**
  - ➢ Position the subject such that it fills the frame, leaving a featureless object four inches (ten cm) away from the lens. Then, to release the camera, half-press the button.
  - ➢ The focus will stay at infinity if tracking is being used.
  - ➢ In the manual focus mode, manually set the focus to infinity.
- **Record the reference information:**
  - ➢ To record the reference data for the Image Dust Off setting, press the shutter release button.
  - ➢ Pressing the shutter release button will cause the display to switch off.
  - ➢ The camera may not be able to capture the reference data if the reference object is too bright or dark. The camera will return to the screen from Step 1 once a warning appears. Press the shutter release button once more to choose a new reference object.

Warning: Cleaning the Image Sensor

Reference data acquired earlier in the procedure cannot be utilized with any photos taken after the image sensor has been cleaned. Choose the [Clean sensor and then start] option if you do not want to utilize the Image Dust Off reference data with the current photos.

Risks Associated with Obtaining Image Dust-Off Reference Data

- ⊹ Using an FX-format lens with a minimum focal length of 50 millimeters is recommended.
- ⊹ Make sure the image is completely expanded before employing a zoom lens.
- ⊹ When a DX lens is placed on the camera, it is impossible to get Image Dust Off reference data.

- You may compare photos shot at various aperture settings or with different lenses using the same reference data.
- Reference photos cannot be seen in PC picture-editing software.
- When looking at reference images, a grid will show on the camera display.

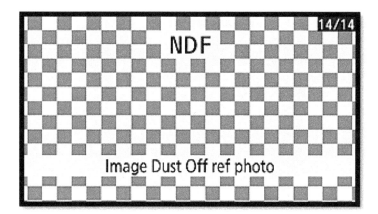

Mapping Pixels

One maintenance procedure that can enhance the camera's image sensor's performance is pixel mapping. If you see unexpected bright spots in your images, it is very useful. Here's how to do pixel mapping and some things to consider:

Power Source and Compatibility Requirements

- **Compatibility:**
  - Pixel mapping works flawlessly with Z-mount lenses.
  - If you're using lenses with an FTZ II mount, you'll need to utilize an FTZ adaptor.
- **Options for Power Sources:** You have the following choices to make sure the camera has enough power when pixel mapping:
  - **Completely Charged Battery:** Before beginning, make sure your camera's battery is completely charged.
  - **EH-7P AC Adapter:** While pixel mapping is taking place, use the EH-7P AC Adapter to keep your battery charged.
  - An extra attachment that is compatible with the EH-5d, EH-5c, or EH-5b AC chargers is the optional EP-5B Power Connector.
  - **Optional EH-8P AC Adapter:** This adapter may be used with a UC-E25 USB cable that includes Type-C ends on both sides for a reliable power supply.

How to Begin Pixel Mapping

- Verify that the lens on your camera is suitable (either an FTZ-adapted lens or a Z-mount lens).
- To avoid power outages, connect the camera to a reliable power source.
- Click the [Start] button to start the procedure.
- The camera screen will display a notification alerting you to the beginning of the pixel mapping procedure.

Warnings for Pixel Mapping

- **Don't Use the Camera:** When pixel mapping is underway, refrain from using the camera for other purposes.
- **Preserve Power:** Throughout the pixel mapping procedure, avoid shutting off the camera or unplugging the power supply. Map data may become damaged or incomplete as a consequence of interruptions.
- **Temperature Considerations:** Pixel mapping could not work if the camera is overheated. Before attempting again, let the camera cool down.

Image Remark

You should write a message whenever you capture fresh photos. To see the notes, launch NX Studio and choose the [Info] tab.

Comment Input

Your message may include up to 36 characters. A text box will appear if you push when the [Input remark] option is selected.

Attaching comment

Photographs shot with [Attach comment] "ON" will already have comments added.

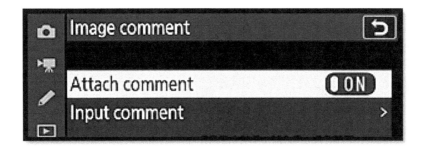

Photo Information

+ On the photo information screen, you may see remarks under the heading "Other shooting data."
+ To see the [Other shooting data] page, choose [Playback display options] and [Other shooting data] from the Playback menu.

Information of Copyright

Provide rights information when fresh photos are taken. The NX Studio [Info] tab contains copyright information.

Copyright/Artist

Enter the rights author's name (up to 54 characters) and the photographer's name (up to 36 characters). Click [Artist] or [Copyright] to launch a text-entry box.

Attach Copyright Information

The copyright information will be appended to subsequent photographs when [Attach copyright information] is [ON].

Warnings: Copyright Details

Make sure [OFF] is chosen under [Attach copyright information] if you want to lend or rent the camera to someone. This prevents the name of the artist or the owner of the rights from being used without their permission. Additionally, you should keep the copyright and artist boxes empty.

+ Nikon disclaims all liability for any problems or damages resulting from the use of the [Copyright information] function.

Viewing Copyright Information

- The [Copyright info] page's image information box shows the copyright facts.
- The [Copyright info] page may be accessed by selecting [Playback display options] from the playback menu, then [Shooting data] and [Copyright info].

About IPTC

As shown below, you may add or change IPTC settings on the camera and apply them to newly taken   images.

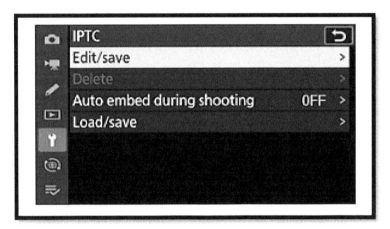

Preset creation, renaming, editing, and copying

- To see a list of options that you can modify or save, highlight [Edit/save] and click the ⊙ button.
- Choose a setting and hit the ⊙ button to update or change it. Select "Unused" and hit the ⊙ button to create a new configuration.
  - ➢ [Rename]: Modify the preset's name.
  - ➢ [Edit IPTC information]: See the configuration you have chosen.
  - ➢ You may customize the fields that you choose.
- Give the copy a name, choose the location where you want to store it, and click OK.

Eliminating Presets

Press [Delete] to remove a preset, and then click the ⊙ button to confirm.

Presets embedding

A list of options will show up once you choose [Auto embed while filming] and hit the
⊙button. If you choose a preset and click OK, it will be used in all of your subsequent
photos. Choose [Off] to disable embedding.

Examining IPTC Information

   - On the [IPTC data] page, integrated settings are shown in the photo information
      screen.
   - Select both [Shooting data] and [IPTC data] from the Playback menu for the
      [Playback display choices]. The [IPTC data] page will appear as a result.

Using a Memory Card to Copy Presets

Go to [Load/Save] > [CFexpress/XQD card slot] or [SD card slot], choose [Copy to card],
and then press ⊙ to transfer IPTC settings from the camera to a memory card. Select the
desired preset and the desired spot (1–99) to copy to the card, and then click "OK."

Using the Camera to Copy Presets

The camera may save up to ten settings. Go to [Load/save] > [CFexpress/XQD card slot]
or [SD card slot], choose [copy to camera], and then press ⊙ to transfer IPTC settings
from a memory card to a specific location on the camera.

   - Press "OK" after selecting a preset to bring up the "Select Destination" list. As an
      alternative to clicking "OK," click ⊖ (?) to see the highlighted option. Click OK
      to go to the [Select destination] list if you're satisfied with the configuration.
   - After selecting a location and clicking OK, a window allowing you to name the
      setting will appear. To save a configuration to the camera, choose it and click
      "OK."
   - The camera may save up to three XMP/IPTC presets that are stored in XMP
      format on a computer in addition to the 10 settings mentioned above. When the

music is playing, the XMP/IPTC options are not shown. Additionally, they cannot be transferred from the camera to a memory card.

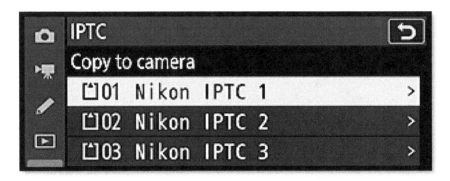

Warnings: IPTC Data

+ Only regular Roman characters and digits are readable by the camera. On devices other than computers, any additional characters may not show up correctly.
+ Pre-set names may include up to eighteen characters.
+ The maximum number of characters permitted in each place is stated below. If a preset is created on a computer with a name longer than eighteen characters, all characters beyond the eighteenth will be eliminated. Any further characters that exceed the allotted space will be eliminated.

The IPTC

The International Press Telecommunications Council, or IPTC, created a standard to facilitate and expedite the exchange of picture information across various publications and organizations. By ensuring that the required information is included in picture exchanges, this approach helps to streamline the process.

Function of the connection (headphone/remote cord connector)

Connect a device to the headphone/remote cable⍾/✐ connection to set it to use.

↳ When [Auto switch] is selected, the camera will automatically determine whether the attached device is the optional MC-DC3 remote cable or headphones. [Auto switch] should remain selected for regular operation.

↳ Choose [Headphone] manually if the headphones do not function properly with the [Auto switch] option (for example, when using headphones with a 4-pole connector).

Options for Voice Memos

You may adjust the recording and control of voice memos using these options.

Control of Voice Memos

By going to Custom Setting f3 [Custom controls (playback)], you may change the [Voice notes] controls.

Options:

↳ **[Press and hold]:** To record a voice memo for up to 60 seconds, hold down the control for a few seconds.

↳ **[Press to start/stop]:** To begin recording, press the control; it will automatically end after 60 seconds or upon pressing it again.

Sounds from the Camera

The camera has a number of sound options that you may change.

Beep On/Off

The beep sound may be turned on or off.

↳ **The camera will beep if [On] is chosen while doing the following actions:**

➢ When the countdown on the self-timer starts.

➢ Following time-lapse video capture, focus change, or interval timing.

➢ Note that this only works if [Release] is chosen for Custom Setting a2 [AF-S priority selection] or if AF-C is configured as the focus mode. The camera will either focus in picture mode or not focus in photo mode if neither of these requirements is satisfied.

↳ To silence touch control beeps, choose "Off (touch controls only)." For other purposes, the buzzer will continue to sound.

The volume

Both the sound produced when the shutter is released and the beep's loudness may be changed.

Pitch

To adjust the beep's tone, choose [High] or [Low] from the menu. There is no way to alter the shutter sound frequency.

Mode of Silence

The electrical shutter is activated when [ON] is chosen. This stops the mechanical shutter from making noise and causing "shutter shock."

- The camera is not entirely quiet while in silent mode, but all other noises are muted. Even with narrower apertures (f-numbers greater than f/5.6), you could still hear noises like autofocus or aperture adjustments.
- Regardless of the Custom Setting d5 [Shutter type] selection, the automatic shutter will be used.
- Even if you adjust the camera sound settings, beep noises will be muffled and the speaker will remain silent.
- In quiet mode, the frame progress rate can decrease.
- When quiet mode is selected, the picture shooting menu does not provide options such as [Long exposure NR] and [picture flicker reduction].
- Flash units that are not necessary will not function.
- **Be aware of the following possible problems that might show up on the screen or in pictures while you're in quiet mode:**
  - Bands or flickering in scenes illuminated by sodium, mercury vapor, or fluorescent lights.
  - Motion-related distortion (if the camera moves during the shot, it may result in distorted subjects or a distorted picture overall).
  - Bright spots, moiré, color fringing, or rough edges.
  - Bright patches or bands in situations where there are fast light sources, such as flashing signs or rapid strobe lights.

Photographers should exercise caution when it comes to safeguarding the privacy and image rights of their subjects, even when quiet mode lowers noise levels.

The Timer on Standby

A sound will play when the sleep timer begins or finishes, even if [ON] is selected for [Silent mode]. Go to Custom Setting c3 [Power off delay] > [Standby timer] and choose [No limit] to turn off the standby timer.

Touch-Based Controls

Touch features on the LCD panel may be turned on or off. During playback, you may optionally choose between left/right or right/left flicks to go to the next image.

Turn on and off touch controls

Touch features may be completely disabled or activated. To enable touch features only while playback is underway, choose [Playback only].

Mode of Gloves

The touch screen becomes more sensitive when set to [ON], which facilitates glove usage.

Mode of Self-Portrait

When the display is turned to the self-portrait position, the camera will not automatically transition to self-portrait mode if [OFF] is chosen.

HDMI

HDMI Configuration

You may change the HDMI output's parameters by selecting the [HDMI] option in the configuration menu.
- **[Output resolution]:** For the output resolution, you may choose from [Auto], [2160p (progressive)], [1080p (progressive)], [1080i (interlaced)], or [720p (progressive).
  - ➢ Even if a recorder capable of handling 1080i resolution is attached, the video will not be delivered at that resolution if "Auto" is chosen for "Output resolution". If you want the output in an interlaced format, choose [1080i (interlaced)].
- **[Output range]:** It is advised to leave the option on "Auto" to align the output range with the HDMI device since different RGB video signals may be handled by

73

different HDMI devices. You may manually choose if the camera is unable to determine the proper range:

> **[Limited range]:** Compatible with devices that provide RGB video between 16 and 235. This option might be useful if shadows aren't detailed enough.
> **[Full range]:** For gadgets that process RGB video data in the range of 0 to 255. Choose this option if shadows seem too bright or "washed out."

+ **[Output shooting info]:** This setting allows you to control whether the HDMI device displays shot information. Selecting [ON] will preserve the video on external cameras together with the icons and other information that is presented.
+ **[Mirror camera info display]:** When an HDMI device is attached, this option controls whether the camera monitor screen remains on.

> To save battery life, the screen will switch off when [OFF] is selected.
> [Mirror camera info display] will always be [ON], however [Output shooting info] cannot be turned off.

+ **"Output Resolution"**

> The camera automatically determines if the external recorder supports the chosen frame size and rate if "Auto" is selected for [HDMI] > [Output resolution]. Otherwise, the camera will adapt to a frame rate and size that works. If there are no appropriate parameters, the output will halt.

Frame size/frame rate	Output resolution/frame rate search order
[3840×2160; 60p]	1080/60p → 2160/30p → 1080/30p
[3840×2160; 50p]	1080/50p → 2160/25p → 1080/25p
[3840×2160; 30p]	2160/30p → 1080/30p
[3840×2160; 25p]	2160/25p → 1080/25p
[3840×2160; 24p]	2160/24p → 1080/24p
[1920×1080; 120p] [1920×1080; 30p ×4 (slow-motion)] [1920×1080; 24p ×5 (slow-motion)]	1080/120p → 1080/60p → 1080/30p
[1920×1080; 100p] [1920×1080; 25p ×4 (slow-motion)]	1080/100p → 1080/50p → 1080/25p
[1920×1080; 60p]	1080/60p → 1080/30p
[1920×1080; 50p]	1080/50p → 1080/25p
[1920×1080; 30p]	1080/30p
[1920×1080; 25p]	1080/25p
[1920×1080; 24p]	1080/24p

- The video will be delivered at the desired resolution if you pick an output resolution other than "Auto". We'll stop the HDMI broadcast if:
  - The output quality that was chosen is more than the frame size.
  - The selected output quality is too high for the recorder.

Options for "Output Resolution" Frame Rates Apart from "Auto"

The following adjustments will be made to video recording speeds such as 120p, 100p, 60p, or 50p if the frame rate of the external camera is incompatible:
- **120p:** It will first decrease to 60p. It will change to 30p if that isn't supported.
- **100p:** If incompatible, it will initially decrease to 50p and then to 25p.
- **60p:** This will become 30p.
- **50p:** 25p will be used instead.

Frame Rates for "1080i (Interlaced)" as the "Output Resolution"

- Films that were shot in 120p, 60p, 30p, or 24p will be re-played at 60i.
- Films shot at 25p, 50p, or 100p will be re-played at 50i.

Frame Rates for "720p (Progressive)" as the "Output Resolution"

- Films recorded in 120p, 60p, 30p, or 24p will be re-played in 60p.
- Films recorded at 25p, 50p, or 100p will be re-played at 50p.

Zoom

- You may zoom in on the camera screen while recording by using the X button, but the video output that is transferred to the external player will remain unaffected.

About Bit Depth and YCbCr

- The YCbCr value and bit depth of the video that is delivered to external HDMI devices may be changed using the [Video file type] and [Frame size/frame rate] options in the menu.

Video file type	Frame size/frame rate	YCbCr and bit depth
H.265 10-bit (MOV)	3840×2160 60p/50p/30p/25p/24p	4:2:2 10-bit
	1920×1080	
H.265 8-bit (MOV)	3840×2160 60p/50p/30p/25p/24p	4:2:2 8-bit
	1920×1080	
H.264 8-bit (MP4)	1920×1080	4:2:2 8-bit

Recording to External Recorders with a Bit Depth of 10 Bits

ᛖ The HDMI signal with the greater bit depth will only be received by HDMI recorders that have a bit depth of 10 bits.

The Tone Mode and HDMI Output

ᛖ The tone mode you pick will also be applied to the HDMI video output when you select [Video file type] in the video recording menu. You will want equipment that supports HDR (HLG) if you choose [HLG].

Control of External Recording

ᛖ **Camera controls may begin and stop recording on the external recorder by choosing [ON] for [External rec. cntrl (HDMI)] in the video recording menu.**
  ➤ Find out whether your recorder accepts control from other formats by contacting the manufacturer.
  ➤ When the period specified in Custom Setting c3 [Power off delay] > [Standby timer] passes, the camera screen will automatically shut down, terminating the HDMI output. You may set the [Standby timer] to [No limit] or a longer duration to continue recording on an external device.

Priority of USB Connection

You may choose which function the camera wishes to utilize first when you connect it to your computer via USB.
  ᛖ **[Upload]:** Despite the camera being linked to a computer, nothing will appear on the monitor's screen. When the camera release button is pushed halfway, the display comes on, although upload rates may be slowed down.
  ᛖ **[Shooting]:** Even with the camera attached to the computer, the screen will remain visible. File speeds might decrease.

Marking for Conformance

The main function of this item is to show all of the many international standards that the camera conforms with. It has been included here since Nikon has the right to alter the title when updating the firmware. After every update, it could be possible to print fresh labels, similar to the one on the camera's base.

Details of the Battery

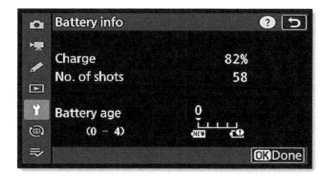

Accessing the Battery Info displays the following information:
- **Charge:** This shows the percentage of the battery's current charge, ranging from 100% to 0%.
- The quantity of shots indicates the number of times the battery has been used since the previous charge. Because the shutter may have been pushed for other purposes, such as presetting the white balance, it can be more than the number of actual photos shot.
- **Battery life:** Batteries ultimately need to be changed since they lose capacity over time. The battery's state is indicated by this symbol:

> - 0 indicates a **new battery.**
> - 1, 2, 3 shows a battery that is **losing power.**
> - 4 indicate a battery that is **fully discharged** and needs replacing. When charging at temperatures **below 41°F (5°C)**, battery life may be temporarily reduced, but charging above **68°F (20°C)** restores its normal performance.

The number of shots

[No. of shots] indicates the number of times the shutter has been pushed on the camera. During manual white balance testing, for example, the camera may push the shutter button without actually capturing a photo.

Battery Charging at Low Temperatures

Batteries may lose their power in cold weather. Even with a brand-new battery, the [Battery age] number may momentarily rise from 0 to 1 if it is charged at temperatures lower than 5°C (41°F). However, once charged at 20°C (68°F) or above, this will revert to normal.

Power Delivery via USB

The camera may be charged using the AC charger that comes with it or by using a USB power source to connect it to a computer. **USB power may be used to power the camera with little to no battery depletion.**

   + **[ON]:** Connected devices will transmit power when the camera is turned on. The camera will continue to run even after it is switched off if the memory card light is on or Bluetooth is enabled.
   + **[OFF]:** No power from connected devices will be used by the camera. The camera can only be powered by inserting the battery.
   + When the camera is linked to an external power source, a USB power supply symbol appears on both the control screen and the shot display.

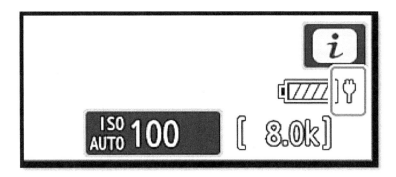

USB Power Delivery for Computers

   + Make sure the computer has a USB Type C port in order to power the camera. Make use of the Type-C ports on both ends of the optional UC-E25 USB cable.
   + Depending on the model and specs, some PCs could not have adequate power.

"Power Delivery" vs. "Charging"

Whereas "power delivery" refers to the use of electricity to operate the camera, "charging" refers to the use of power just to charge the camera battery. **The following**

scenarios demonstrate how external power may be used to either charge the battery or power the camera:

Option selected for [USB power delivery]	Power switch	External power source used for
[ON]	On (standby timer active)*	Power delivery
	On (standby timer off)	Charging
	Off	Charging
[OFF]	On (standby timer active)*	—
	On (standby timer off)	Charging
	Off	Charging

+ Memory card access or Bluetooth updates may continue to function even when the power switch is off.
+ When plugged into a computer, an EH-7P charging AC adapter, or an EH-8P charging AC adapter, EN EL15c or EN EL15b batteries will begin to charge. Be careful to connect to PCs or the EH-8P using the UC-E25 USB cable.

Saving Energy (Photo Mode)

To save battery life, the screen will go off in picture mode 15 seconds before the idle timer expires.
+ **[ON]:** Turns on energy-saving mode, which may cause the displays to update more slowly.
+ **[OFF]:** This energy-saving setting is turned off, however the camera screen will still dim just before the idle timer expires.

Please be aware that even with [ON] chosen, energy conservation may not always be successful. **In these situations, energy conservation won't work:**
+ If you choose [No limit] or a Custom Setting c3 [Power off delay] > [Standby timer] delay of less than 30 seconds.
+ When photographing oneself.
+ While zooming in
+ When connecting the camera to another device via HDMI
+ When transferring data using a USB connection
+ When the camera is plugged in with an AC adapter.

Lock for Slot Empty Release

Select whether the shutter may be opened if the camera is not using a memory card.

	Option	Description
LOCK	[Release locked]	The shutter cannot be released when no memory card is inserted.
OK	[Enable release]	The shutter can be released with no memory card inserted. No pictures will be recorded; during playback, the camera displays [Demo].

Menu Settings: Save/load

These configurations are stored:

- **Playback Menu:** You may change settings such photo review, delete after burst, show after burst, and rotate tall using the playback display choices.

- **Photo Shooting Menu:** This menu allows you to name your files, choose the region of the photograph, and adjust ISO sensitivity, white balance, quality, size, and other options. Vignette control, diffraction correction, auto distortion adjustment, metering, vibration control, flash mode, AF-area mode, focus reduction, flash bracketing, silent photography, active D-lighting, long exposure NR, high ISO NR, and vignette control are additional options.

- The Video Recording Menu allows you to choose the ISO sensitivity, image area, frame size, frame rate, movie quality, and video file name. Additionally, you may change the focus mode, AF-area mode, flicker reduction, metering, vignette control, diffraction adjustment, auto distortion correction, vibration reduction, electronic VR, image control, black balance, and active D-lighting. You may also adjust the frequency response, headphone volume, microphone sensitivity, and timecode (but not the timecode origin) settings.

- **Custom Settings Menu:** Everything except d3 is included in this menu.

- The setup menu lets you set up language, time zone, information display, non-CPU lens data, clean image sensor, date and time, image comments, copyright information, beep options, touch controls, HDMI settings, location data (but not position), wireless remote control options, and Fn button assignments for remote controls. You may control the slot empty release lock as well.

- **Recent Settings/My Menu:** This area displays the current tab, all of the items in My Menu, and any recent modifications.

Menu Settings Saving and Loading

- **Save Menu preferences:** An SD card may be used to save your preferences. The settings cannot be stored if the card is full; an error message will show. Only other cameras of the same kind may use saved settings.

- **Load Menu Settings:** Before you can access the [Load menu settings] option, you must insert a memory card containing the stored settings in order to load them from an SD card.

Reset every setting

- With the exception of [Language] and [Time zone and date], most settings will return to their initial settings upon reset. Additionally, copyright information and user-generated comments will be deleted. Setting changes cannot be undone unless you save them before resuming using the [store/load menu settings] option.

Version of the firmware

You can see whether your camera has the most recent firmware update. You may use the memory card to upgrade the firmware of the camera if it has an updated version of the software on it.

Updates for Firmware

- **Computer:** The Nikon Download Center offers fresh software upgrades for PC users. For updates and other information, visit the website.
- **Smart Device:** The SnapBridge app will alert you when an update is available if you connect your phone to the camera. The update may then be pushed to the memory card of the camera using the phone. Refer to the SnapBridge app's online support for more information. According to certain users, SnapBridge may not provide alerts for updates that are available on the Nikon Download Center.

The Menu for Photo Shooting

Quality of Image

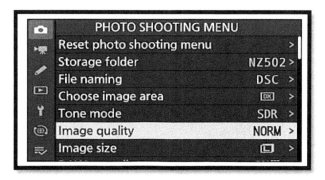

(Star) [RAW + JPEG/HEIF fine], [RAW + JPEG/HEIF fine] [Raw + JPEG/HEIF normal (star)], [Normal] JPEG/HEIF basic (star) in RAW format, JPEG/HEIF basic in RAW format: For every image, create two copies: one in JPEG or HEIF format and one in NEF (RAW) format.

- Both a JPEG copy and a NEF (RAW) picture will be saved by the camera if you choose [SDR] in the [Tone mode] photo shooting menu. The camera will store a HEIF and a NEF (RAW) duplicate when [HLG] is chosen in the [Tone mode] menu.
- To improve the appearance of your JPEG or HEIF copy, use the choices that have a star next to them. Select the alternatives without a star if you would rather keep your JPEG or HEIF files around the same size.
- The camera will only show the JPEG or HEIF copy of images captured in two distinct formats when only one memory card is attached.
- Removing the JPEG or HEIF copy will also remove the NEF (RAW) image if the shot was taken with a single memory card or with two cards with [Overflow] or [Backup] selected in the photo shooting menu under [Secondary slot function].

The RAW file format

- Images in NEF (RAW) format may be recorded. For your photographs, choose either the JPEG or HEIF format; "Fine" offers the highest quality, followed by "Normal," and "Basic" offers the lowest.
- The images are stored in JPEG format when [SDR] is chosen for Tone mode. The HEIF format is used to save images captured with [HLG] selected for Tone mode.
- Choose the choices that have a star next to them for the highest quality image. Choose alternatives without a star if you wish to maintain the same size for all of your files.

About the image size

- To adjust the size of fresh photographs, choose [Image size] from the photo shooting menu. Additionally, you may choose [Large], [Medium], or [Small] for formats other than NEF (RAW).

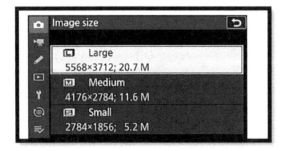

⊥ By default, NEF (RAW) images are captured at the [Large] size.

Image area	Image size	Size (cm/in.) when printed at 300 dpi
[DX (24×16)]	Large (5568 × 3712 pixels)	Approx. 47.1 × 31.4 cm/18.5 × 12.4 in.
	Medium (4176 × 2784 pixels)	Approx. 35.4 × 23.6 cm/13.9 × 9.3 in.
	Small (2784 × 1856 pixels)	Approx. 23.6 × 15.7 cm/9.3 × 6.2 in.
[1:1 (16×16)]	Large (3712 × 3712 pixels)	Approx. 31.4 × 31.4 cm/12.4 × 12.4 in.
	Medium (2784 × 2784 pixels)	Approx. 23.6 × 23.6 cm/9.3 × 9.3 in.
	Small (1856 × 1856 pixels)	Approx. 15.7 × 15.7 cm/6.2 × 6.2 in.
[16:9 (24×14)]	Large (5568 × 3128 pixels)	Approx. 47.1 × 26.5 cm/18.6 × 10.4 in.
	Medium (4176 × 2344 pixels)	Approx. 35.4 × 19.8 cm/13.9 × 7.8 in.
	Small (2784 × 1560 pixels)	Approx. 23.6 × 13.2 cm/9.3 × 5.2 in.

Settings for ISO Sensitivity

Modify the photo's ISO strength settings. There are extended settings of 0.3, 0.7, 1, or 2 EV over ISO 51200, which is comparable to ISO 204800, and you may choose between ISO 100 and 51200. Both Auto and SCN shooting modes provide the [Auto] option.

⊥ **Auto ISO sensitivity control:** Press the [ON] button to activate auto ISO sensitivity control. The user-specified ISO sensitivity setting won't alter if [OFF] is used.

⊥ **Maximum sensitivity:** To prevent the sensitivity from becoming too high, choose a maximum ISO level.

⊥ **Maximum sensitivity with [Flash]:** Select the ISO value that gives your images the sharpest quality if you're using an extra flash.

⊥ **Lowest shutter speed:** To avoid underexposure, you may choose the lowest shutter speed in P and A modes at which auto ISO sensitivity will kick in. The range of selectable speeds is 1/166,000 to 30 seconds.

➢ With "Auto" selected, the camera will use the focal length of the lens to determine the lowest shutter speed. For instance, the camera will choose a quicker minimum shutter speed when a long lens is mounted in order to minimize blur from camera motion and guarantee crisp shots.

⊥ **Auto Shutter Speed Adjustment:** To change the automatic shutter speed, tap the ⟳ button and choose "Auto." You may adjust the auto shutter speed for sharper images by selecting faster or slower minimum shutter speeds, particularly when taking shots of moving objects. Quicker settings aid in minimizing motion blur.

- The shutter speed may decrease below the chosen minimum speed to get the proper exposure if the [Maximum sensitivity] option is unable to produce an acceptable exposure.

About Focus Mode

[Auto-switch AF mode]

- Only available in picture mode, the camera employs AF-S for still images and AF-C for video images.

AF-S [Single AF]

- Apply to subjects that are motionless. The focus point will change from red to green and focus will lock if you click the shutter-release button midway through the focusing process. The focus point will flash red and the shutter release will be turned off if the camera is unable to focus.
- The shutter can only be released at default settings if the camera can focus (focus priority).

[Continuous AF] AF-C

- For topics that move. While the shutter-release button is halfway engaged, the camera continually adjusts focus in response to variations in the distance to the target.
- The shutter may be released at default settings regardless of whether the subject is in focus (release priority).

[Full-time AF] AF-F

- The focus point will shift from red to green and focus will lock when the shutter-release button is pushed halfway. The camera continually modifies focus in reaction to subject movement or compositional adjustments.
- Only in video mode is this option accessible.

MF [Focus manually]

Attention by hand (Manual focus). Regardless of whether the subject is in focus or not, the shutter may be released.

AF-area Mode

The [AF-area mode/subj. detection] item in the i menu or the [AF-area mode] items in the picture shooting and video recording menus are the ways to choose the AF-area mode.

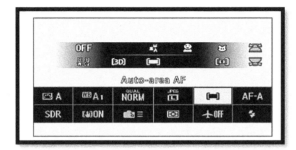

[PinPoint AF]

- Although focusing may be slower than with single-point AF, it offers a narrower focus point than single-point AF, enabling more accurate focus on a particular area of the frame.
- It is advised for close-ups, studio product photography, and static things like buildings.
- Only accessible in picture mode when the focus mode [Single AF] is used.

[One-point AF]

- Ideal for stationary subjects, the camera focuses on a spot that the user selects.

[Dynamic-area area AF (S)], [Dynamic-area AF (M)], [Dynamic-area AF (L)]

- If the subject temporarily departs the chosen point, the camera will follow focus based on information from nearby points. Otherwise, the camera focuses on a point that the user selects.
- Only accessible in picture mode when [Continuous AF] or [AF mode auto-switch] is chosen.
- Perfect for topics that are difficult to frame or moving, like athletes.
- **The focus area's size may be set to S (small), M (medium), or L (large):**
  - ➤ [Dynamic-area AF (S)] works best for things that move reliably, such racing cars or runners.

> ➤ [Dynamic-area AF (M)] works well with subjects that move erratically, such football players.
> ➤ [Dynamic-area AF (L)] works well with things that move quickly, such birds.

[Wide-area AF (S)], [Wide-area AF (L)]

- Choose for snapshots, moving images, or things that are challenging to picture with single-point AF.
- It has features similar to single-point AF, but it focuses on a larger area.
- Wide-area AF is helpful in video mode for smooth focus when panning, tilting, or recording moving subjects.
- The camera will give priority to the closest subject if subjects are at different distances from it.
- The focus points for [Wide-area AF (L)] are larger than those for [Wide-area AF (S)].

[C1 Wide-area AF], [C2 Wide-area AF]

- Allows you to choose the focus areas' dimensions (measured in focus points).
- Helpful when you are aware of the dimensions and form of the space that will be utilized for concentration beforehand.
- To set the AF-area size, press and hold the J button after choosing [Wide-area AF (C1)] or [Wide-area AF (C2)]. To choose height, press buttons 1 and 3, and to choose width, press keys 4 and 2.
- There are 60 picture mode choices and 50 video mode settings available.

[Tracking in 3D]

- Tracks concentrate on a chosen topic as it passes across the frame.
- The camera will begin following the target if you place the focus point over them and push the shutter-release button halfway. To stop tracking and go back to the previous focus point, let go of the button.
- Release the shutter button to recompose the image with the subject back in focus if they move out of the frame.
- Available in picture mode when [Continuous AF] or [AF mode auto-switch] is chosen.

[Tracking the subject AF]

+ Tracks focus on a chosen subject by placing the focus point over the subject and initiating tracking by partly pushing the shutter-release button or J. To choose the center focus point and stop tracking, press J once again.
+ Only video mode is accessible in this mode.

[Auto-area AF]

When you don't have time to manually choose the focus point, such in portraits, snapshots, or impromptu photographs, the camera automatically recognizes the subject and chooses the best focus point.

The Release Mode

To choose what occurs when you push the shutter-release button down, utilize the [Release mode] option in the picture shooting menu.

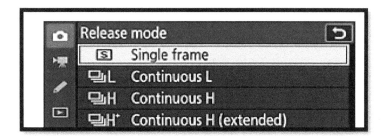

+ **[Single frame]:** The camera captures a single image when the shutter-release button is pressed.
+ **[Continuous L]:** The camera captures images at a predetermined pace, known as "continuous L."
  ➢ Using Custom Setting d1 [CL mode shooting speed], you may adjust the rate between [1 fps] and [7 fps].
+ **[Continuous H]:** The camera captures images at a maximum rate of 10 frames per second when you hold down the shutter-release button.
+ **[Continuous H (extended)]:** The camera can capture up to 15 frames per second while the shutter-release button is pushed.
+ **[C30]:** When the shutter-release button is pushed, this mode records 30 frames per second.
+ **[Self-timer]:** Delay the picture capture by using the self-timer.

Photographic Burst Shooting Display

When both the low-speed and high-speed burst modes are in use, the shot display presents a live view through the lens.

Frame Advance Rate

The camera's settings determine the maximum frame rates for [Continuous H] and [Continuous H (extended)].

Warnings: Photography in Burst

- Depending on the card's performance and the surrounding conditions, the memory card access light may stay on for a few seconds to a minute. To prevent damage or losing any unrecorded photographs, do not remove the memory card while the light is on.
- The memory card access light will remain on until all of the photos in the buffer have been saved if the camera is switched off.
- The shutter button will not work if the battery dies while there are still images in the buffer, but the images will be stored on the memory card.

Fast Frame Recording plus (C15/C30)

- For [Release mode], choose [C15 or C30] to take pictures at 30 frames per second (high-speed frame capture+).

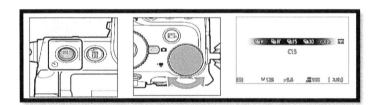

- For high-speed picture capture+, the maximum burst time is around four seconds.
- The saved pictures could also include pictures taken during pre-release capture, which is when the shutter release button was partially depressed. To regulate the amount of buffer stored, you may modify the Pre-Release Capture settings using Custom Setting d3. After you push the shutter button, you may also choose how long the burst lasts.

> ➢ The touch camera only allows you to capture one picture at a time. Click the shutter-release button to take quick pictures.

Self-timer

Before snapping the picture, you may specify a delay using the self-timer. You have the following choices to choose from:

- ✦ **Self-timer delay:** It may be modified to 2, 5, or 20 seconds, although by default it is 10 seconds. When the camera is on a stand or other support, or if you're too sluggish to use the cable release, this helps avoid camera wobble.
- ✦ **Shot count:** After the self-timer countdown is over, you may program the camera to capture one to nine images. This function is excellent for group photos since it guarantees that everyone is smiling and has their eyes open in the picture.
- ✦ **Time between photos:** You may choose a time interval between shots if you select two to nine images. Options include 0.5, 1, and 2 seconds; a 3-second interval is best for flash usage since it gives the flash time to recharge before the subsequent shot.

Active D-Lighting

The purpose of active D-lighting is to assist you manage the contrast in your photos. Occasionally, a scene's light spectrum is too wide for the camera's sensor to fully capture. Despite the Nikon Z camera's great dynamic range, there are certain circumstances in which the sensor may still be unable to capture enough light, or you may just want to lessen the contrast of the picture. Active D-Lighting improves the dynamic range of the picture by lowering contrast, especially by maintaining highlights and opening up shadows. This leads to better balanced exposure and more detailed shadows, particularly in situations with high contrast. One drawback is that more noise could show up in shadowed places, although this is less of a problem than with earlier versions thanks to the camera's superb noise management.

Levels of Active D-Lighting

You may choose the amount of contrast reduction you want in your picture using Active D-Lighting's six levels:

- Auto (A)
- *Extra high (H)**
- High (H)
- Normal (N)
- Low (L)
- Off (no Active D-Lighting)

89

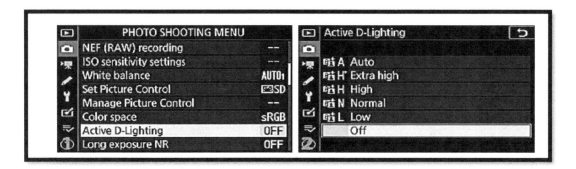

Choosing a Level of Active D-Lighting

Use these procedures to choose an Active D-Lighting level:
- From the menu, choose Active D-Lighting.
- To confirm your selection, tap the option or hit OK after selecting your chosen setting (or off).

The Impact of Active D-Lighting on Your Image

Active D-Lighting is particularly useful for highlighting features that are obscured by shadows brought on by too much contrast. Additionally, it prevents highlights from becoming completely white and losing their detail. **This is how it works at various levels:**
- Low levels will somewhat lessen highlight intensity and emphasize more shadow detail.
- A small HDR effect may be produced by high levels (such as *Extra high (H)**), which would result in a reduced contrast overall but more pronounced details in the highlights and shadows.

You can see how the algorithm gradually opens up the shadows and tames the highlights in a rosebush scene with significant contrast—heavy shade and dazzling highlights—thereby reducing the overall contrast. The picture may seem somewhat HDR at the H* setting, with a more balanced dynamic range.

Recommendations for Settings

It's crucial to try out different Active D-Lighting levels to choose your favorite. Some users may not appreciate the lower contrast results since it lessens visual contrast. Additionally, you could detect additional noise in such regions while extracting shadow details. This feature is especially helpful for JPEG shooters since it helps construct the picture with the optimum contrast from the beginning, which is crucial because JPEGs are difficult to edit after shooting. Active D-Lighting may help control contrast and maintain details in both the highlights and shadows in high contrast situations, such taking pictures in full sunshine. Active D-Lighting helps retain shadow detail and keeps highlights from becoming too harsh, particularly when utilizing flash in a low-light setting, which is useful in circumstances like wedding ceremonies when you need to preserve detail in the bride's clothing.

Concluding remarks

To see how the camera reacts, try Active D-illumination in a range of illumination settings, including strong contrast and low contrast, and at all levels. Doing so will help you determine how to utilize this feature most effectively for your purposes and will give you a better idea of how it might be used to various shooting circumstances.

Control of Vignettes

The natural vignette effect, which is a slow darkening of the corners of images that may happen with certain lenses, can be lessened or enhanced using the Nikon Z50 II's Vignette Control submenu.

Options for Vignette Control

- Off: Turns off vignette correction, maintaining the organic vignette effect for a more styled or artistic appearance.
- Low, Normal, and High: These options brighten the image's darker areas by applying different amounts of correction. In order to remove the vignette effect, Low applies a slight correction, Normal is standard, and High applies a greater correction.

Take caution: Vignette control

JPEG photographs may include "noise" (fog) or over-processing near the border of the frame that produces changes in peripheral brightness, depending on the scene, shooting circumstances, and lens type. Additionally, the intended effect could not be achieved by modifying preset Picture Controls or Custom Picture Controls from their initial values. Observe the outcomes on the display after taking test shots. The video recording menu is affected by changes made to [Vignette control] in the picture shooting menu, and vice versa.

About Auto Distortion Control

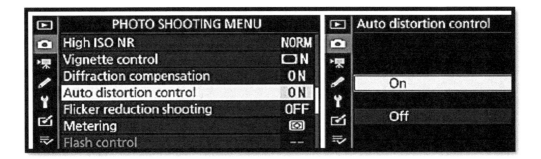

To get rid of barrel distortion with wide-angle lenses and pin-cushion distortion with long lenses, choose [ON]. But be aware that certain lenses could choose [ON] for you automatically, rendering this choice grayed out or inaccessible. Any modifications made to [Auto distortion control] in the menu for taking pictures will also be reflected in the menu for recording videos, and vice versa.

Noise Reduction from Extended Exposure (NR)

When shooting at a shutter speed of less than one second, turn on [ON] for Long Exposure NR to cut down on "noise" (fog or bright spots) in your images.

+ After the photo is taken, noise is reduced. While the picture is being processed, the control panel will flash "Job NR" and the shot display will read "[Performing noise reduction]."

+ While noise reduction is underway, no further photos may be taken. Your whole photography session will take longer since the picture processing time will double.

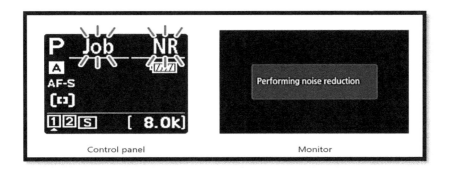

| Control panel | Monitor |

When the exposure is complete, a timer will show on the control panel if the shutter speed is set to "Bulb," "Time," or any other setting that is slower than 30 seconds. The remaining processing time will be shown by this timer.

Warning: Noise Reduction for Extended Exposure

- ⊹ If the camera is turned off before processing is complete, there may be incomplete noise reduction. The picture will still be stored, however.
- ⊹ It's crucial to understand that Long Exposure NR may greatly increase the overall exposure duration. For instance, the camera will take a black frame (a second exposure with the lens covered) for an additional 10 seconds after a 10-second exposure, for a total of 20 seconds throughout the capture process.
- ⊹ For photographers who wish to avoid motion blur or catch fast-moving objects, this prolonged duration may be an issue.

Long Exposure NR is often not immediately accessible when shooting in RAW format. Rather, the camera applies it to JPEG photos. To give you greater control over the finished picture, post-processing software could include noise reduction features that you can use on RAW files afterward.

Suggestions

- Long Exposure NR might be a useful feature if you often use long exposures and want to minimize noticeable noise in your photos. It is preferable to disable this option and manually perform noise reduction using specialist software if you shoot in RAW and would rather have control over the process during post-processing.
- Only when shooting in JPEG or other formats that use in-camera processing will Long Exposure NR is available.

The High ISO NR

Increasing the ISO sensitivity on your camera lets it catch more light, which is useful when there is little light. Increasing the ISO, however, may also result in digital noise, which shows up in the picture as hazy or speckle patterns. To reduce this noise, noise reduction methods are used either during or after the picture collection process. **High ISO NR reduces the amount of apparent noise in the following ways:**

- The camera analyzes the image and uses noise reduction algorithms to minimize visible noise when High ISO NR is turned on.
- This often entails smoothing down the picture, which may cause some fine features to be lost.
- The camera's algorithms try to balance lowering noise and preserving picture clarity.

The High ISO NR options that are available are

- [High], [Normal], and [Low]; these settings eliminate noise to varying degrees. The noise reduction rises with increasing setting, however finer details may be blurred.
- [Off]: The camera only applies noise reduction when it senses that it is necessary. Compared to selecting [Low] or higher, the noise reduction level is lower.

Remember that the effectiveness of high ISO NR varies based on the manufacturer of the camera, the ISO setting, and the particular noise reduction technique being used. The picture may look less crisp if noise reduction is used excessively, particularly in regions with tiny details. You have additional options for noise reduction if you shot in RAW format. All sensor data is preserved in RAW files, so you may manually perform noise reduction using specialist software during post-processing.

Flash Control

Any wireless remote flash units or extra flash units connected to the camera's extension shoe may have their settings changed.

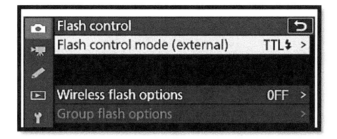

Mode of Flash Control

For flash units that are compatible (SB-5000, SB-500, SB-400, or SB-300), choose a flash control mode and flash level.

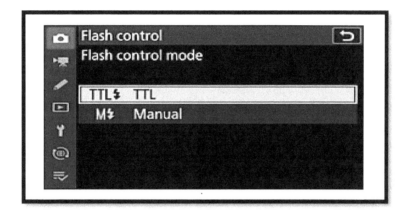

+ The flash control mode you choose will determine the possibilities available.
+ If you have a flash unit that is not on the list, you will have to change the settings on the flash unit itself.

Options for Wireless Flash

When utilizing compatible devices like the SB-5000, SB-500, or WR-R11a wireless remote, turn on the wireless flash control settings. This enables you to operate several remote flash units simultaneously.

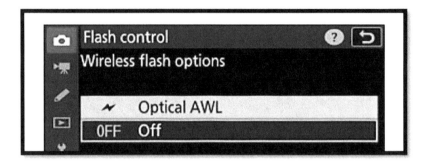

Flash Control via Remote

- To remotely modify flash settings, use the Remote Flash Control option.
- For each group (A, B, and C), you may modify the flash output. You can also choose Remote Repeating to enable numerous flashes while the shutter is open or Quick Wireless Control for instantaneous changes.

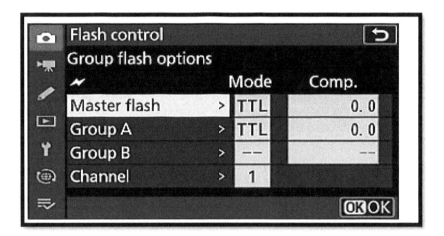

Flash Mode

With this option, you may choose the flash mode that best suits your requirements as a photographer:

- **[Fill flash] (Front-curtain sync):** Usually the default setting. This setting fires the flash to fill up shadows when using P or A exposure mode. Auto FP high-speed sync is offered for quicker shutter speeds, and the shutter speed will be adjusted between 1/200s and 1/160s.

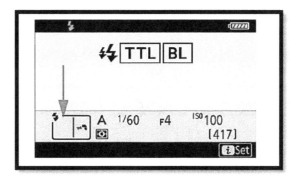

✦ **Rear Curtain Sync Mode:** The flash starts as soon as the shutter's rear curtain starts to close. This is helpful when using flash to create motion trails, which are often employed while photographing moving scenes at night.

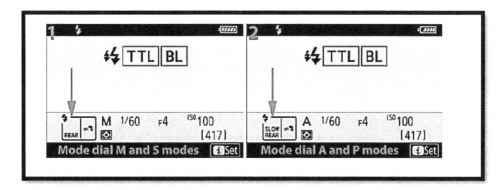

✦ **Slow Sync option:** This option uses a slower shutter speed to blend ambient light and flash. It aids in accurately capturing the backdrop while illuminating the subject with flash. Depending on your desire, you may choose between front-curtain sync and rear-curtain sync.

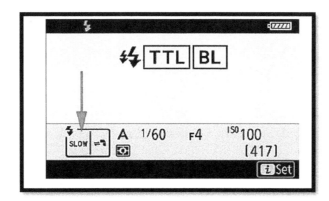

+ **Red-Eye Reduction Mode:** To lessen the possibility of red-eye in the picture, the camera fires a sequence of pre-flashes to cause the subject's pupils to contract. When direct flash is required in low light conditions, this is often used.

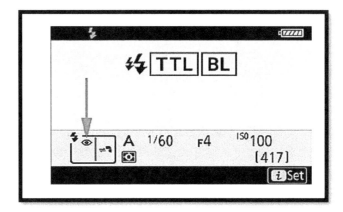

+ **[Slow sync + red-eye]:** For low-light portraiture, this method combines slow sync with red-eye suppression. A tripod is advised since this technique employs slower shutter speeds and may result in blur from camera shaking.

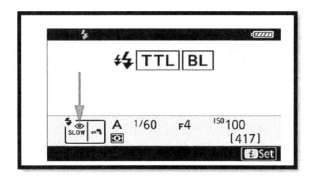

Extra Auto settings

+ **[Auto]:** When the subject is backlit or there is inadequate illumination, the flash activates automatically as required.
+ **[Auto + red-eye reduction]:** To reduce red-eye in low light, flash fires when necessary while using red-eye reduction.
+ **[Auto slow sync]:** This is comparable to slow sync, but only when necessary does the flash ignite.
+ **[Auto slow sync + red-eye]:** This option automatically combines red-eye correction and slow sync.

↓ **[Flash off]:** Completely turns off the flash.

Flash Compensation

You may adjust the amount of power that the flash unit emits. We call this procedure "flash tuning." You may adjust the camera's metering settings to improve or worsen the flash if you utilize flash correction. This may be accomplished simply varying the flash signal's intensity. You may adjust the flash exposure in this setting to get the desired lighting effect while maintaining the harmony between the natural light in the room and the flash. Typically, stops or portions of stops, such +1.0, +0.5, 0, -0.5, -1.0, and so forth, are used to display the flash correction number. The flashlight becomes brighter as the flash intensity is increased by plus signs (+). Conversely, when the value is -, the flash strength drops, resulting in a less dazzling light.

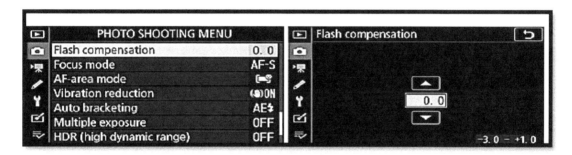

In actual life, flash correction works as follows:
↓ **Positive Flash Compensation:** This technique allows you to increase the amount of light that the flash emits if you use a flash and discover that your subject is too dark or there isn't enough light. You should take these actions if you discover that utilizing a flash exacerbates the aforementioned problems. This ensures that the lighting is perfect and helps the subject stand out more.
↓ **Negative Flash Compensation:** You may need to reduce the flash's intensity if the image is very brilliant or the illumination is too harsh. The flash loses some of its intensity when it is set to negative. This might improve the flash's performance by producing more natural light.

There are other methods to adjust the flash, including using the settings on the camera, specific buttons or knobs, and more. Depending on the kind of camera, this may vary. Usually, you have to utilize a dedicated flash unit or be in a flash mode (such as TTL or manual) in order to use the flash correction settings. Remember that adjusting the flash settings simply alters what the flash is emitting; it has no effect on the brightness of the image. Always keep this in mind. To alter the exposure overall, exposure adjustment is required. This feature allows you to adjust the camera's ISO, shutter speed, and aperture.

The Menu for Playback

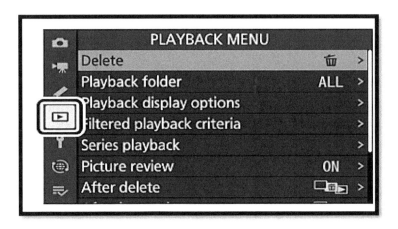

Eliminate

There are four alternatives available for this menu item:

1. [Selected images]: Remove You may find a selection of photographs under [Selected photos].
2. [Candidates for deletion]: Images that have been identified as "candidates for deletion" may be removed.
3. [Photos taken on specified dates]: Remove every picture taken on the given dates.
4. [All pictures]: Remove every image from the folder that is selected as the [Playback folder] in the playback option.

If you insert two memory cards, you may choose which one will be used to remove the images. Using the Protect option is one technique to safeguard an image. Pressing the i button during Playback brings up the i menu, where you may find this. Over the image, a cover key symbol will appear. Pictures that have been marked with the key symbol will not be deleted when using this option to remove images. Remember that removing photographs this way takes a lot longer than wiping all the data on the memory card using the Format command. Choosing Format is thus often quicker than choosing Delete: It's also a better technique to restore your memory card to its original state, which was empty.

Playback folder

- **[Folder name]:** During playback, images from every folder with the chosen name are shown. The [Storage folder] > [Rename] option in the picture shooting menu allows you to rename folders.
- **[All]:** Shows images from every folder while it is playing.
- **[Current]:** During playback, only images from the current folder will be seen.

Options for the playback display

- **[Focus point]:** Choose this option to see the location of the focus point at the time the photo was captured.
- **[Mark first shot in series]:** This feature, when activated, will display an icon and a number indicating the number of shots taken during each burst.

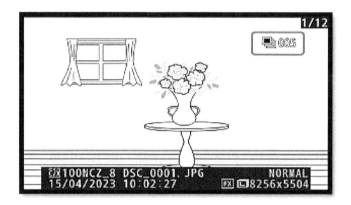

The following choices are available when you push or use the DISP button to show the specified information:

- [Exposure info]
- [Highlights]
- [RGB histogram]
- [Shooting data]
- [Overview]
- [None (picture only)]
- [File info]

Options shown on the full-frame playback [Shooting data] display include:

- [Basic shooting data]
- [Flash data]
- [Picture Control/HLG data]
- [Other shooting data]
- [Copyright info]
- [Location data]
- [IPTC data]

About series playback

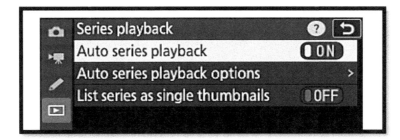

- **Automatic playback of series:**
  - ➢ If [ON] is chosen, the first image in the burst will be shown in full frame for a few seconds before the next photos start playing automatically.
  - ➢ After the last image in the burst has been shown, playback stops.

Options for Auto Series Playback

- **[Loop playback]:** To play back the shown burst group repeatedly, set this to [ON].
- **[Wait before playback]:** After the first picture in the burst group is shown, choose the delay period before auto series playback begins. The alternatives that are available are:

- [Long]
- [Normal]
- [Short]
- [Start immediately]

102

- **[Auto series playback speed]:** You may choose the auto series playback speed as follows:
- **[5 fps], [15 fps], [30 fps]:** Replay at the chosen pace.
- **[At the speed of the current release mode]:** Playback takes place at the pace of the current release mode.
- The playback speed will be 3 frames per second if the self-timer or single frame release option is used.

Display series as individual thumbnails

Only the first shot from each burst will show up in the thumbnail list when [ON] is selected. A c symbol and a figure indicating the total number of shots in the burst will be used to identify the initial image in each burst.
- During full-frame playback, every image in each burst will be seen.
- Selecting [ON] for [List series as single thumbnails] enables the playback i menu's [Manage series] option.

Review of the Image

Picture evaluations show the picture you just shot in the electronic viewfinder (EVF) or on the monitor of your camera. Each photo will be shown immediately after it is taken if this option is enabled. You may check the picture for quality and usefulness. You won't see every photo until you click the Playback button since picture review is disabled. This may help you preserve battery life if you utilize Live View often. If you want to see each picture once you snap it, you must activate this option. You may choose how long each picture stays on the monitor before shutting off by navigating to Custom Setting Menu > Timers/AE lock > Power off delay > picture review. You may adjust the duration of this image custom display review time to show photographs for anything from two seconds to ten minutes. Image Review may be set up in three different ways. **Let's examine each of them:**

- **On:** The image appears on the display or EVF whenever the shutter is released. The screen will return to its previous state when the review period has ended. Through the EVF, the camera will show the picture that your eye is looking at. If you hold the camera away from your eye, it will show the picture on the rear monitor instead. You can't take any more photographs when reviewing images on the EVF until you either examine the image for the timeout duration, which is by default 4 seconds, or you half-press the shutter release button to end the review and resume regular viewing. If you are shooting in spurts or need to be able to take another shot immediately, you may not want both the monitor and the EVF to have image review activated. In the following situation, you could do better.

- **On (only for monitoring):** only displays the image on the rear screen. This works more like a DSLR since you can evaluate photos immediately after they are shot. Because you may disregard the display, this mode may be the most helpful if you need to snap more pictures rapidly while utilizing the EVF.
- **Off:** When the monitor or EVF is off, the picture you just shot is not visible. You must hit the Playback button in order for the current display (Monitor or EVF) to display it.

After deletion

A new picture will appear on the camera's monitor if you remove an image while it is being played back (image review). The After deletion feature allows you to choose which picture will be shown after you remove an image. Either the current picture or the previous one may be erased by the camera, or it can determine whether you were scrolling ahead or backward and use that information to choose which image should be shown after you remove one. **Three options are available in the menu after deletion:**

- **Show Next:** The camera will show the subsequent picture on the memory card if you remove an image that wasn't the last one on the card. If you remove the last picture off the card, the previous image will be shown since there isn't a following image. The camera's typical operation will be shown next.
- **Show previous:** If you remove a picture that is not the first image on the memory card, the previous display will be erased. If you remove the first picture from the memory card, the camera will show the following image because there isn't a preceding image.
- **Continue as before:** This odd environment demonstrates the versatility of computerized camera technology. If you scroll to the right (the order in which the photos were taken) and choose to remove one, the camera will utilize the Show Next technique to show the next image. If you happen to be scrolling to the left when you delete a photo, the camera will utilize the Show Previous method instead, which is the contrary of the sequence in which the images were shot.

After a burst, display

Select whether the image that appears immediately after a continuous mode burst of pictures is the first or final shot in the burst. Only when [Off] is selected for [Picture review] in the playback menu will this option be active.

Document the orientation of the camera

The camera's angle of view at the time of the photo is recorded if [ON] is selected. Images are automatically rotated during playback on a computer or camera, depending on the orientation data that was captured.

Take caution: Document the orientation of the camera

Those who take sweeping images or tilt their cameras up or down may not capture the proper camera orientation.

Automatically Rotate Images

The playback display will automatically rotate to match the camera orientation if [ON] is selected. For instance, "tall" images will rotate to show in "tall" orientation when the camera is held in "wide" position, and "wide" images will rotate to display in "wide" orientation when the camera is held in "wide" orientation.

Warnings: Auto-rotating images

When you look at images, they do not automatically rotate, even if [ON] is selected for [Auto-rotate pictures]. Rotation is not automatically applied to images taken with [Record camera orientation] set to [OFF] in the playback menu. Photos will appear on the replay display because they were taken in the "wide" orientation.

The Menu for Custom Settings

You may use Custom Settings to adjust your camera's operation to help it live longer. These settings are a little more reliable. Depending on where you shoot, you will probably make several changes to the Photo Shooting and Video Recording menu selections. However, you may capture photographs using Custom Settings. To make it simpler to line up tall or broad forms, you may choose to activate the viewfinder grid display or assign a frequently used function to the Fn button. Some of the choices are basic adjustments that might be helpful in certain shooting scenarios. The camera is

often simpler to operate with many features. Simply choose the tab in the camera's settings to see the Custom Settings choices.

Priority Selection for AF-C

➕ **Release:** Pressing the shutter release button allows you to shoot a photo immediately (release priority). When the release button is completely depressed, this option opens the shutter even if the camera is not in crisp focus. AF-C continuously focuses and refocuses while autofocus is enabled, which might result in a less-than-sharp image. This choice is more crucial than getting the focus accurate when shooting a photograph, especially in photojournalism or scenarios where you need to respond fast.

➢ Yes, you will still be able to fine-tune your focus with this option; it just ensures that you will capture a photo even if autofocusing isn't finished. (You don't want to miss the protester smashing a pie into the Governor's face!). You probably stood still with the shutter release half-pressed while the Z50 II checked the focus of the shot.

➕ **Focus + release:** The first image in each series will be focused before the others in continuous-release mode if the subject is dark or lacks contrast. The first image in a series is often focused before the others.

➕ **Focus:** This implies that the camera must be in focus in order to shoot photographs. Until the image is sharp, the shutter is not pushed. This is most effective for subjects that are not moving rapidly. The Z50 II won't capture a photo until the focus is locked. However, AF-C will monitor your subjects while they are in motion. You may miss a few, but there will be fewer out-of-focus photos.

Priority Selection for AF-S

If AF-S is chosen, you may choose whether the camera can shoot a picture before focusing. AF-C priority option allows you to choose how the autofocus operates while you're in Continuous-servo Focus mode (AF-C). Be sure you understand how to use this feature. If you do not adjust this option appropriately for your photography style, you may end up with some out-of-focus photos. **There are two different options available:**

➕ **Release:** Even if the shutter is out of focus, this makes it fire each time you click the shutter-release button. Until the shutter is released, autofocus is "delayed". If you must snap the picture no matter what, you will have to set the AF-C priority to Release. The shutter button will be pressed even if the camera is unable to concentrate on your subject. You must use your expertise to do tasks like prefocusing or using depth of field to cover the topic in order to ensure that it is in focus. The factory-installed setting is called release.

± **Focus:** If your camera is unable to focus, this option prevents it from capturing a photo. If the shutter is not in focus, the image will not be released. This does not imply that the camera will always concentrate on the appropriate object. The camera won't concentrate on anything until the shutter is released. Nikon cameras are excellent at focusing, so you can often rely on autofocus to function properly with them. This Focus option will significantly improve the chances that your picture is in the right focus. The camera will concentrate on each frame if you utilize the Continuous release mode. The firing may halt if there are moments in the sequence when there is insufficient attention.

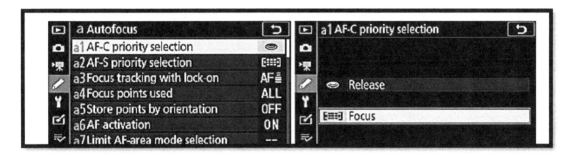

Lock-On Focus Tracking

If you choose AF-C as the mode, you may adjust the speed at which focus changes if anything comes in the way of the subject and the camera.

Blocked Shot AF Reaction

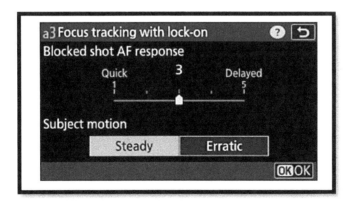

With this setting, you may adjust the Z50 II's response time to short disruptions that might result in obvious shifts in concentration before going back to the "new" topic. A automobile may pass directly in front of the lens if you're photographing a structure from the other side of the street. The Blocked Shot AF Response slider is seen in the image above. The Z50 II may be adjusted to either a short delay to immediately reset when a new subject enters the frame or a lengthy delay to ignore the intruder. If the option is 5 (Delayed), the Z50 II looks away from the object in front of it for a very long period. When photographing sports or other situations where the subject may get distracted for extended periods of time, this option works well. Option 1 will cause the Z50 II to focus immediately. When you adjust the delay between 2 and 4, the amount of delay varies. The intermediate number in this instance, 3, provides you with a pause before the camera focuses again on the next topic. This is often the best choice when shooting sports in any of the continuous modes since the larger delay may reduce AF's accuracy at higher frame rates.

- To maintain the emphasis on your first topic, choose [5] (Delayed).
- Press [1] (Quick) to help you concentrate on what's in front of you.
- Regardless of the AF-area mode choice selected, the blocked shot AF response operates in mode [3].
- The AF-area mode that you may choose is [Auto-area AF]. Mode [3] will then function for the stopped shot AF response when [2] or [1] is selected.

Step Value for ISO Sensitivity

One exposure value or one-third of an exposure value may be used to adjust the ISO sensitivity. The value that is closest to the available ISO sensitivity value will be used if the selected value is not available at that level.

EV Exposure Control Steps

Select the procedures for adjusting the exposure, bracketing, shutter speed, aperture, and flash correction.

- Adjustments to the shutter speed, aperture, and bracketing will be done in 1 EV stages if you choose [1 EV (comp. 1/3 EV)]. Steps of ± EV will be used to adjust the exposure and flash correction.

Simple Compensation for Exposure

Rather of using the +/− Exposure Compensation button, you may use Easy Exposure Compensation to adjust the camera's exposure compensation. To adjust the exposure, you may use the Command dial of your choosing instead. There are three settings for easy exposure compensation: On (auto reset), On, and Off. If the camera is set to "On (Auto reset)" or "On," you may adjust the exposure using the Command dials rather than the +/− button. The +/− button must be used if you want to alter the exposure. For each exposure setting (P, S, A, and M), easy exposure compensation works a little differently.

When you employ the Program (P), Shutter-priority (S), and Aperture-priority (A) modes, they all perform separate tasks. You may still make changes using the standard +/− Exposure compensation button even if Custom setting b2 doesn't alter the Manual (M) mode. The values and their operation are as follows: Activated (auto reset): By setting the Main command dial to Aperture-priority (A) mode or the Sub-command dial to Program (P) or Shutter-priority (S) mode, you may adjust the exposure without using the +/− button while this option is enabled (Auto reset). The aperture or shutter speed is often controlled by the other Command dial.

    ⤷ As soon as you switch off the camera or let the meter go off, the compensation value you entered is reset to 0. For this reason, it is called "Auto reset." The standard +/− Exposure compensation button may be used to establish compensation initially. The compensation is then added or subtracted from the amount you specify using the standard +/- Exposure compensation button when you use the Command dial to establish compensation. The meter returns to the value you specified as compensation, not to zero, when you hit the +/− Exposure compensation button.

On: When the meter or camera is switched off, the adjustment you have established stays in place rather than being reset.

Off: The exposure is only altered via the standard +/- Exposure correction button.

Keep in mind: The degree to which you may fine-tune the exposure using Easy exposure compensation is altered by custom setting b1, which allows you to choose between 1/3 and 1/2 EV step sizes. Additionally, you may adjust the primary and secondary command dials in the Custom Setting Menu (f5). Here, you can adjust the shutter speed, aperture, and compensation.

You can adjust the exposure using either the standard +/- Exposure compensation button or Easy exposure compensation. When exposure correction is in effect, the EVF and Monitor will display a +/- sign.

Face Detection with Matrix Metering

The option to adjust the exposure for the faces of human portrait subjects the camera sees is available when [Matrix metering] is selected. If you set the camera to "ON," everyone in the image will have their exposure changed immediately. This switch may be turned "OFF," which will prevent the exposure setting from checking for faces.

Modify for the Best Exposure

Using this feature, you may alter the exposure setting that the camera has previously set. There are several methods to adjust the exposure for each metering technique. The exposure may be adjusted from +1 EV to -1 EV in 1/6 EV increments. When you move the exposure up, it becomes brighter, and when you change it down, it gets darker. In this example, it's set to 0.

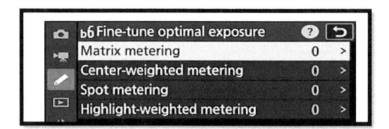

You may choose the precise amount of exposure compensation that will be applied immediately with this extremely useful feature, eliminating the need to adjust it for every image you capture in any of the three metering modes. "My Z50 II always underexposes by 1/3 stop!" is not necessary. "This modification can be performed to the custom menu to solve the problem if it occurs repeatedly."

Maximum Number of Shots per Burst

The maximum number of shots that can be fired in a single burst in continuous release modes can be set to any value between 1 and 200. No matter whatever option you choose, you may shoot as many photos as you want in a single burst if you set the shutter speed in mode S or M to 1 second or less.

The buffer for memory

A Custom Setting called "Max. Shots per burst" allow you to specify the maximum number of shots that can be taken in a burst. The number of pictures that can be taken before the memory buffer fills up and shooting slows down depends on the image quality and other parameters. When the buffer is filled, the camera will show "r000" and the frame advance rate will drop.

The buffer for memory

The number of photos that may be captured in a single burst is controlled by the Custom Setting d2 [Maximum shots per burst]. The number of pictures that can be taken before the memory buffer fills up and the camera slows down depends on the image quality and other variables. The camera will display "r000" and the rate of frame addition will slow down as soon as the buffer is full.

Options for Pre-Release Capture

When the shutter-release button is depressed, you may choose the duration of the burst that record from the end of the memory buffer. Additionally, when the shutter release button is completely engaged, you may choose the longest burst length that will be captured.

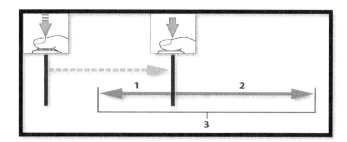

1. Standby Pre-Release Capture (maximum 90 s)
2. A portion of the buffer was written to the memory card during release ([pre-release burst]).
3. Images captured after the release ([post-release burst])
4. Complete burst at high speed

[Pre-release bursting]: In the event that you select a setting other than "None," the camera will buffer frames while the shutter-release button is left partially depressed. When you click the shutter-release button, only the frames that were added to the buffer in the past n seconds—where n is the number you selected for "Pre-release burst"—will be stored on the memory card.

> ⁺ The camera will only capture the images that were saved to the buffer when the button was halfway pressed if the interval between pressing it halfway and pressing it all the way down is shorter than the predetermined time.

[Post-release burst] allows you to choose how long the camera will continue to take images after pressing the shutter release button. Four choices are available: [1 s], [2 s], [3 s], or [Max. You may continue shooting for up to 4 seconds at a time if you choose [Max.]. Selecting a setting other than "None" for the "Pre-release burst" option will result in an icon appearing on your shot display. This is set to "None." The symbol will display a green dot to indicate that buffering is now taking place when you push the shutter release button halfway.

111

+ The ⚠ sign will show and Pre-Release Capture will terminate if you hold down the shutter release button for more than 30 seconds. To resume Pre-Release Capture, lift your finger from the shutter release button and push it halfway again. This lets you continue shooting until the shutter is fully released.

Sync. Options for Release Mode

You may check to determine whether the shutter speeds of the remote cameras match those of the master camera by using the [Connect to other cameras] option in the network menu or an additional wireless remote device.

Mode of Exposure Delay

The shutter doesn't truly release until 0.2 to 3 seconds when the exposure delay mode button is pushed. With the hopes that during the wait, the camera vibrations would cease and the picture will be clearer. **The parameters in exposure delay mode are as follows:**

+ 0.2 s, 0.5 s, 1 s, 2 s, or 3 s: As shown in picture 2, the camera waits between 0.2 and 3 seconds before firing the shutter, depending on the setting you choose. Any vibrations caused by touching the camera may be eliminated before the shutter opens by doing this. Naturally, whether you're shooting an action shot or anything that moves, this won't assist at all. This is a great feature for shooting scenes that don't move.

+ **Off:** This option causes the shutter to operate immediately.

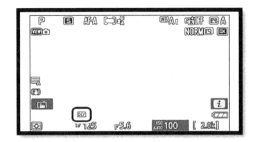

View Everything in Continuous Mode

You may choose full-frame playback during burst shooting in live view while shooting in Continuous Low, Continuous High, or Quiet Continuous mode using this option. If you choose "Off," both the video screen and the monitor's illumination will be off while you shoot continuous pictures.

Release Timing Indicator

- **[Type A]:** For Type A, the screen turns dark as soon as the snap button is let go.
- **[Type B]:** The top, bottom, and sides of the frame display the frame edges when the shutter is opened.
- **[Type C]:** The image will have lines on the left and right when you release the camera button.
- **[Off]:** The release time is not displayed when the camera release button is pressed.

It should be noted that even if the correct option is selected, release time indicators will not appear when the shutter speed is set to a low value.

Picture Frame

Go to the settings and pick [OFF] to eliminate the white line surrounding the shooting photos on the display and viewfinder.

Grid Type

Select a grid for the frames of the shooting display. The selected grid may be shown by placing a "M" next to "b" in the Custom Setting d17 [Custom monitor shooting display] list.

Type of Virtual Horizon

The region of the screen where you will fire should have a faux edge. The selected virtual horizon will appear if you place a "M" next to D in the list for Custom Setting d17 [Custom monitor shooting display].

- **Type A:** A large number representing roll and pitch makes up the display.

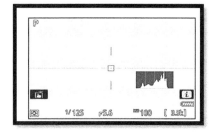

✦ **Type B:** The screen has a roll indication at the bottom and a pitch indicator on the right.

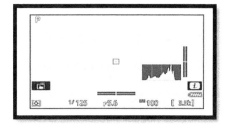

The screen may not display the correct information if you angle the camera very far forward or backward. When the camera is held at an angle that prevents tilt measurement, it will not display the pitch and roll markers or the virtual horizon.

Personalized Shooting Display for Monitors

Press the DISP button to flip between the different displays while you're filming.

✦ Items in bold ([Display 2] through [Display 5]) may be turned on or off by clicking the OK button. You can only view the panels that have a checkmark on them when you hit the DISP button while filming. You are unable to remove the option on [Display 1].

Choose the display-specific option and hit [🕐] to choose the messages that will be shown on displays [Display 1] through [Display 4]. After that, you may highlight items and click the OK button to accept or reject them.

- **[Fundamental shooting data]:** The shutter speed, aperture, shooting mode, and other fundamental shooting details are shown when you click on the "Basic shooting info" button.
- **[Detailed shooting data]:** You may see the white balance, focus mode, AF-area mode, and other specialized shooting information by selecting the "Detailed shooting info" option from the menu.
- **[Touch controls]:** Examine the many settings available to you using touch controls, such as the touch i menu and the touch AF menu.
- **[Virtual Horizon]:** To use it, you must ensure that it is turned on. A Custom Setting called "Virtual Horizon Type" allows you to choose the kind of show.
- **[Virtual horizon]:** To activate the RGB histogram for the virtual horizon, click the "Histogram" button.
- **[Framing grid]:** Before using it, make sure the frame grid is turned on. Here, you may alter the view type in Custom Setting d15, also known as "Grid type,"
- **[Center indication]:** To use the center indicator, position the eyes precisely in the center of the screen.
- **[Display 5]** is comprised only of the shown data; it is not modifiable.
- The procedure may be terminated by pressing the MENU button.

Order of Bracketing

You may choose how the bracketing is done using this parameter. The following are the default settings: Under > MTR > Over (which arranges the images from least to most expose for both ambient and flash exposures); MTR > Under > Over (metered exposure), followed by the image with the least exposure, and finally the image with the highest exposure. The screen's numerals read More Yellow > Normal > More Blue and Normal > More Yellow > More Blue. The white balance is also set in this manner. This is the ideal sequence to take photos if you plan to shoot three or more at once. If you utilize just two images for bracketing, you miss one of the three exposures. The sequence in which the photos are taken is up to you. Select [Auto bracketing] > [Auto bracketing set] from the picture shooting menu. When the [Bracketing order] setting is selected, the [ADL bracketing] option has no effect on the shot order.

Priority for Flash Bursts

When shooting burst shots in the high-speed or low-speed continuous display mode, you may choose whether the extra flash units will show pre-flashes before each image.

- ↓ **[Prioritize frame advance rate]:** Prior to each series' initial shot, the flash unit will perform a monitor pre-flash. The output will then be fixed at the value discovered for the remaining shots. The frame rate decreases less when [Prioritize precise flash control] is selected than when it is.
  - ➢ During burst firing, the shooting display will display an FV lock symbol (**🔒**).

- ↓ **[Make precise flash control your top priority]:** Make accurate flash control your top priority. The flash unit regulates how much light the flash emits after firing a monitor pre-flash before each shot. There may be instances where the pace of frame progression slows down.

Custom Shooting Controls

Both the camera and the lens have the ability to alter what the camera does while it is in image mode. These consist of the sub-selector, the control ring on the lens, and the buttons on the camera.

- ↓ Decide which tasks the tools will do. Pressing the OK button will activate the selected setting.

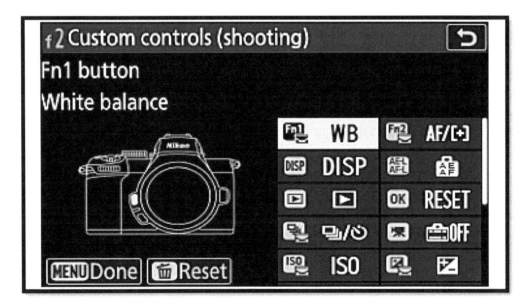

Option	
📷	[Fn1 button]
📷	[Fn2 button]
🔳	[DISP button]
🔳	[AE-L/AF-L button]
▶	[Playback button]
🔳	[OK button]
📷	[Release mode button]
▢	[Video record button]
📷	[ISO sensitivity button]
📷	[Exposure compensation button]
🔳	[Picture Control button]

☷	[Command dials]
🔳	[Lens Fn button]
🔳	[Lens Fn2 button]
🔄	[Lens Fn ring (counterclockwise)]
🔄	[Lens Fn ring (clockwise)]
🔳	[Lens memory set button]
⊙	[Lens control ring]

+ To choose which control to use, you may clear the screen's settings. On the confirmation screen, choose [Yes] after choosing the control you want to reset and pressing the O button. Lastly, click OK to restore the control to its initial configuration. Select any control and hold down the OK button for about three seconds to restore all controls to their initial configurations. Press J after choosing [Yes] on the confirmation box.
+ The positions that are available are listed below. The control determines the roles that may be performed.

117

Dials for commands

The order buttons may be used for these purposes. Select items and push to see the alternatives. Setting for exposure In some settings, [Exposure setting] allows you to swap between the main and sub-command knobs. Press 1 or 3 to switch tasks, then press 4 or 2 to choose a mode. You may press [Focus/AF-area mode selection] to switch between the main and sub-command dial functions. By pressing [Custom controls (shooting)], you may maintain the control you were provided for [Focus mode/AF-area mode] exactly as it is. To choose the function of the zoom display's sub-command dials and alter its duty.

- You may adjust the sub-command dial's function in each mode using this option.
- To zoom in or out using the sub-command key, press [Zoom].

Preserving and Remembering Focus Points

If you give this custom control the [store focus position] command and then push and hold it, it will remember the focus location. You may easily return to the previous stored focus position by clicking on a custom control that contains the [Recall focus position] (sometimes called "memory recall") button. **This function might be useful if you often return to topics at the same subject distance.**

- The [Recall focus position] command may be linked to several controls. To save a position, choose "Save to all" under the "Save focus position" menu. After that, you may go back to that spot using any of the provided tools. Only a specific control may be used to restore them if you selected "Save individually" under the "Save focus position" option.
- You can store where the focus is in any focus mode.
- However, when the lens is removed, the recorded distance is lost.

Warning: Remembering and Preserving Focus Positions

- While shooting in format, information is shown; however, focus points cannot be stored.
- The focus point that is selected when a stored value is retrieved may differ from the focus point that was saved if the temperature changes.
- When you read back the value, the focus point you selected will probably be different if you adjust the zoom.

Custom Playback Controls

You may control what occurs during playback by configuring the camera. What the tools do is up to you. Once you have selected the tool you want to use, press OK.

Lock Control

Lock brightness settings or focal point selection. You may lock the shutter speed in modes S and M using the [Shutter speed lock] option. Select [ON] to do this. This will maintain the current shutter speed.

- "L" symbols will appear on the camera's control panel and shot screen when the shutter speed lock is activated.

Select the [ON] option for the [Aperture lock] setting if you want to maintain the aperture at the same value when in modes A or M. Both the control panel and the camera screen include buttons that resemble the letter "L." When the aperture lock is activated, these buttons are utilized.

[Lock Focus Point]: To keep the focus point selection locked on the presently chosen point, press the [ON] switch button.

- The focus point cannot be locked when [Auto-area AF] is enabled for the AF-area mode.
- If the [3D-tracking] option is selected, the focus point will follow the subject as long as the camera release button is partially depressed.

AF speed

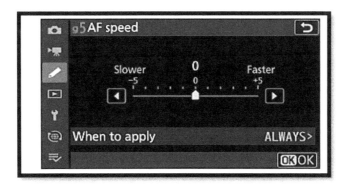

- [Always] in video mode ensures that the camera always focuses at the speed you choose.
- **[Only when recording]:** The focus change speed is only applied while a video is being recorded. The camera may focus quite rapidly at times.

Sounds from the lens

As the AF speed increases, the lens produces a louder sound while focusing. The impact is most pronounced when set to [+5]. Select lower settings if you can't stand the noise.

119

Tracking Sensitivity for AF

You may choose any value between 1 and 7 for the AF tracking strength in video mode.

 ⬥ If you want to keep your initial topic of attention, choose [7] (Low).
 ⬥ The camera will rapidly concentrate on another subject in the same region if the previous subject leaves the designated focus area when it is on the [1] (High) setting.

This is similar to Custom Setting a3: Focus Tracking with Lock-on for movies in still images. One such example is the referee during a football game. When the subject moves or anything else comes in the way, it shows how fast the Z50 II's AF system responds. When the setting is 7 (Low), the Z50 II is not focused on the subject for a considerable amount of time. Use this option for photographing scenes like athletics where there are likely to be frequent and dramatic focus breaks. Option 1, "High," also allow you to instruct the Z50 II to wait a little time before making any adjustments. The middle number, 4, is followed by an additional second or two before the camera refocuses on the next topic.

Zoom Speed in High Resolution

Select the zoom speed for Hi-Res Zoom. This option is only available if Hi-Res Zoom is assigned to a control using either of the [Fn1 button], [Fn2 button], [Lens Fn ring (clockwise)], or [Lens Fn ring (counterclockwise)] choices for Custom Setting g2 [Custom controls].

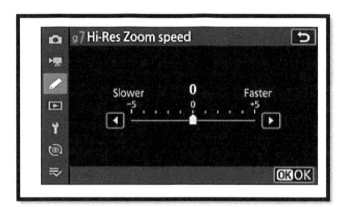

Personalized Shooting Display for Monitors

In video mode, choose a monitor display by pressing the DISP button. To choose or disregard the items shown in [Display 2] through [Display 4], press the OK button. When you use the DISP button while filming, you can only view the screens that are ticked off. [Display 1] cannot be unchecked.

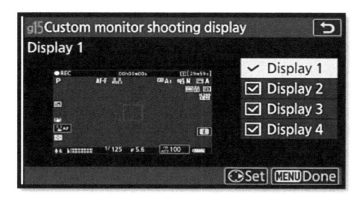

From Displays 1 through 4, choose the choice that matches the sign you want to choose, and then click the ⊙ button. After that, you may highlight the item and click OK to decide whether or not to choose it.

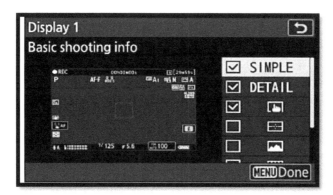

- ♦ **[Basic shooting info]:** Examining the shutter speed, aperture, shooting setting and other crucial shooting details.
- ♦ **[Detailed shooting info]:** See the white balance, AF-area mode, focus mode, and other relevant shooting details.
- ♦ **[Touch controls]:** View tools that can be accessed via touch controls, such as touch AF and the i menu.
- ♦ **[Virtual horizon]:** Choose [Virtual horizon] to switch on the virtual horizon. You may choose the show type using Custom Setting d17 [Virtual Horizon type].
- ♦ **[Brightness information]:** Examine a waveform or histogram for specifics on brightness. Custom Setting g14 [Brightness information display] allows you to choose the kind of display.

121

- **[Framing grid]:** Select the frame grid by going to [frame grid]. In Custom Setting g13 [Grid type], the user may choose the display type.
- **[Center indicator]:** The crosshairs need should be seen in the center of the image.
- To stop, press MENU.

Personalized Viewfinder Shooting Display

- Press the DISP button to choose a viewfinder display in video mode.
- To choose or reject items shown on [Display 2] or [Display 3], press OK. Holding down the DISP button while shooting allows you to view just those displays that have a checkbox next to them. It is not possible to uncheck [Display 1].
- To choose the sign that shows on screens [Display 1] through [Display 3], click on the desired selection and then click ⊙. After that, when you highlight an item and click OK, you may decide whether to pick it. With the exception of [Touch controls], the Custom Setting g15 [Custom monitor shooting display] (g15: Custom Monitor Shooting Display) contains the same choices as this one.
- To finish, press MENU.

REC Frame Indicator in Red

If [ON] is chosen, a red border will surround the shooting display, and this will remain in place while video clips are being saved. You won't miss any photos since you'll know when the recording begins and ends.

Recent Settings Menu /My Menu

We have the option to personalize a menu that only displays the functions we use most often, as well as one that displays the features that have changed lately. Because you will add different camera functionalities to the menu than I or others would, configuring My Menu for each camera will be unique. I often move between the Exposure Delay and Custom Setting modes. To avoid having to go through all of the Custom options and attempt to remember where it was, I added the Exposure delay mode to My Menu. I may just choose Exposure Delay mode from My Menu if I wish to utilize it once again. I don't need to search for it; I can do it fast. I seldom ever utilize Recent Settings. I have the control I want thanks to My Menu, my own completely configurable menu. Since the Recent Settings menu is a camera-controlled menu system that updates itself automatically, you can't make many changes. In contrast, My Menu is a private collection of links to the options I use most often. It may be fully configured. My Menu may have items added or removed at any moment. Even the items you use most often may be rearranged so they are at the top. You are now proficient with My Menu. To include items in My Menu:

My Menu

My menu is my menu! You can add, delete, or rank (move up or down on the menu) almost any camera option on one of the primary menus. I don't have to go through the main menu system to locate the service when I utilize My Menu. Since I often place my most-used features in My Menu, it's excellent to have it immediately.

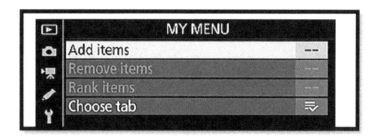

My Menu is the last option on the camera's menu system. A list with a checkmark in the center serves as its symbol. **There are just the following menu choices shown when you initially visit My Menu:**

- Add items
- Remove items
- Rank items
- Choose tab

Let's take a closer look at each of these menu options.

Add Items menu

Before you can add an item to My Menu, you must locate it. Find the setting you want to add by navigating through the options. Put that setting's address in writing. You could do this via the Add Items menu, but I find it more difficult to locate what I'm searching for if I don't already know where it is. Is it in one of the Shooting Menus, the Custom Setting Menu, or the Setup Menu? It may take longer than necessary if you don't first write down the locations of the items you want to add to My Menu.

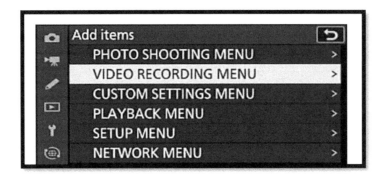

After locating the object you want to add and noting its location, do the following actions:

- Select Add Items from the My Menu's menu. As you can see, Active D-Lighting and Set Picture Control have been added to My Menu. Let's add one more item.
- To the right is a menu list that you may utilize. All of the camera's primary menus are shown on the Add Items screen, with the exception of the Recent Settings and My Menu menus. I want to add exposure delay, which is my favorite setting.
- The Custom Setting Menu has the exposure delay mode. We have to scroll down and then right to reach it.
- We can now see the Custom Setting Menu and Custom Settings using e. After selecting "Shooting/display," move your cursor to the right. As you can see, not all of the Custom options are shown in figure 2. You may also see Custom Settings f and g by scrolling down.
- All we have to do is choose the item and hit or touch OK. Once it is finished, the camera will go to the Choose position screen.

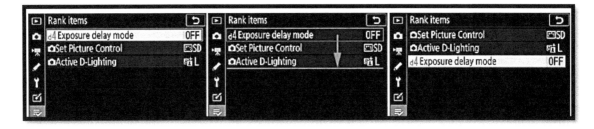

- Since I've already added a couple more items to My Menu, I only need to decide which order I want them to appear in. The new d4 Exposure delay mode option is at the top as it is the most recent. Set Picture Control will remain in its current location as I shift it down two rows.
- You just need to scroll down to relocate the presently selected item. The d4 Exposure delay mode option is surrounded by a yellow box. A yellow line scrolls

down the list with each scroll. The yellow marking indicates where I want to relocate the d4 Exposure delay mode. I just click the OK button after selecting the location and placing the yellow underline there. After a brief message box stating "Saved," the screen returns to the original My Menu page, where everything is configured as I would want. The d4 Exposure delay option is now at the very bottom of the list, as you can see in figure 3.

Remove Items

Let's examine how to delete things now that I've covered how to add them. I can reach the Set Picture Control menu on the camera by hitting the i button and choosing it from the i Menu. Therefore, I believe that the i Menu's Set Picture Control feature is preferable than My Menu's. To make room for anything else in one of the 20 spots, I'll remove it from My Menu.

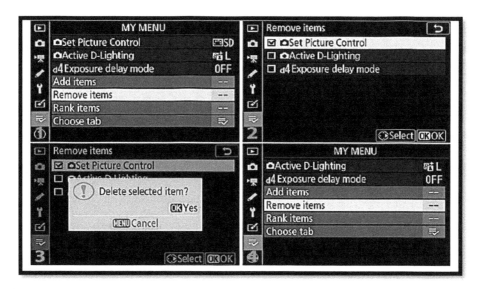

Use these procedures to remove items from My Menu:
- Select "Remove items."
- Several checkboxes are available for selection on the Remove items screen (picture 2). Any boxes you tick will be removed when you press or touch OK. By high-selecting the line item you want to remove and using the Multi-selector pad to scroll right, you may check the boxes. Like a switch, a line item will be checked or unchecked as you scroll right. You may also use your fingertip to touch the box to toggle a checkmark on or off.
- Verify the settings you want to remove, and then click OK. "Delete selected item?" is the question that displays in a little white box. Third picture.

125

⁎ The Set Picture Control setting is removed from My Menu if you touch or press OK (Yes). After a short display of the "Done" popup window, the camera returns to the My Menu screen. If you decide you don't want to remove anything, you may cancel by clicking the MENU button. As you can see in the picture 4, Set Picture Control is no longer available.

Sort Items

Adding new items to My Menu is similar to ranking things. In My Menu, an item may be moved up or down using the straightforward "Rank items" selection. You can move the My Menu items you use most frequently to the top of the list.

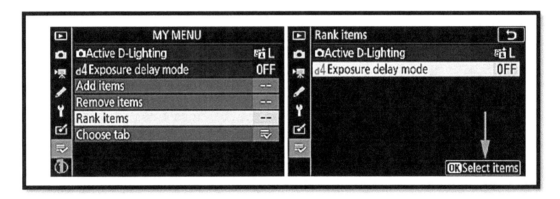

Do the following in order to rank things:
⁎ Select the items to rank.
⁎ All of the items in your My Menu will now be displayed on the Rank items screen. The mode I use the most is this one: Mode of Exposure Delay (d4). As a result, it will be shifted to the top. Touch or press OK. choose things and then choose the one you wish to transfer.
⁎ The item you selected will have a yellow highlight, such as "Exposure delay mode." Pressing up on the Multi-selector pad will move the yellow positioning underline to the top of the list.
⁎ Press or touch OK to select the new location. After that, the d4 Exposure delay mode will take precedence over the others.

Select Tab

By selecting the Choose tab, you can navigate between Recent Settings and My Menu. The Choose tab selection is the last menu option in both menus.
To go between Recent Settings and My Menu, follow these steps:
⁎ Select the Choose tab from My Menu's bottom.

- You may now choose between Recent Settings and My Menu. After selecting "Most Recent Settings," click "OK."
- At this point, the main menu screen will display the Recent Settings screen rather than the My Menu. Take note that, like My Menu, Recent Settings has a selection tab at the bottom. Modifications made recently are displayed in the Recent Settings menu. Your camera will show a different list of items than mine. When you navigate up or down in the Recent Settings panel, the most recent 20 changes will appear. The Choose tab option is all you will see if you have never modified any of the camera's menu items. The Recent Settings menu will display the changes you make to other menu items as they happen.
- To come back to My Menu, click the click tab and hit the OK button. It's evident that this is a cyclical motion. You may flip between the two menus by utilizing the Choose tab option. This makes one menu the final choice on the main menu screen of the camera, replacing the other menu.

Settings Suggestion: As you can see, My Menu offers you excellent control over a completely personalized menu that is all yours. You may configure it anyway you wish by choosing from the options in the main menus. My Menu can help you save a lot of time when searching for your top 20 selections. Remember that after 20 changes, the next setting you use will move everything down one spot if you choose to use Recent Settings. The final item on the list will simply disappear. Now let's take a closer look at Recent Settings.

Recent Settings

Making advantage of Recent Settings is simple. You may see the past 20 menu adjustments you made to your camera from this menu. All menu selections that are changed are stored in a temporary place called Recent Settings. If you make any changes to your camera that isn't already reflected in the Recent Settings menu, they will be added. If there isn't space at the bottom for more than twenty things, the oldest item at the top of the list will be replaced with the new one. This could be helpful if you're looking for something on the main menus that you know you've recently changed but can't recall where it is.

Configuration suggestion: If you would want a more permanent menu for your preferred camera settings, use the My Menu system for the Recent Settings Menu. I would prefer to have direct control over which settings I can access quickly without having to search for them, even though the Recent Settings Menu is helpful. My menu is my choice!

CHAPTER FIVE
UTILIZING YOUR CAMERA TO SHOOT VIDEOS

By flicking a switch labeled "Photo/Video mode" to the right of the viewfinder, you may record videos. Press the red Video button on top of the camera, just southwest of the shutter release button, once the mode dial has been moved to the green Auto position to enter Video mode. This will produce a basic, casual video. The recording will begin. Press the Video button one again to end. All you have to do to obtain quality video is that.

Checklist for Video Recording

As you become more proficient in sophisticated video production and filmmaking, keep the following list in mind. **While some of these subjects are more focused on creating movies, others are recaps of what you already know about taking still images in format.**

- There are still. While filming a video clip, you may capture a cropped, high-resolution still by completely depressing the shutter release. While you are filming your video, there won't be any breaks or missing still photos. The still picture is cropped to match the 16:9 movie aspect ratio and stored at the same resolution as the movie frame size using the JPEG quality setting. This results in a 2MP picture in HD mode with 1920x1080 pixels and an 8MP image in UHD (4K) mode with 3840x2160 pixels.
- If the Continuous release mode is selected, just one picture will be captured when you push the image release button during video recording. The Z7 II allows for 50 individual photographs to be captured during video recording, but the Z6 II only allows for 40.
- There is no flash. You can record video and take still images, however when the flash option is set to Movie, you can't utilize the flash.
- **Compensation for Exposure**. Three levels, each plus or minus three EVs, are available for adjusting the exposure during filming. (Remember that you have five EV increments of plus or minus for still shots.)
- **Dimensions Matter.** Depending on the quality you choose, each video clip may have a maximum size of 4GB and a maximum duration of 29 minutes and 59 seconds. One movie might consist of over eight different files, each 4GB in size. The precise number of files and their durations may vary depending on the frame size and frame rate you choose. Your memory card's speed and capacity may

further limit its size and length. Up to three minutes may be spent on each slow-motion video recording.

+ **Select the appropriate card**. Use a fast XQD or CFexpress card if at all possible. Because full HD video may demand a transmission rate of 28 Mbps, HD video 56 Mbps, and 4K video 144 Mbps, if you insist on using a slower card, the recording may end after a minute or two. No matter what, use a memory card with at least 32GB of capacity. Some older XQD cards have a 16GB capacity, but they most likely won't be quick enough for the High-Quality level.

+ When filming, I exclusively use CFexpress memory cards with 128GB and 256GB. Some of the cards I use are from the Sony G series and the ProGrade range. They can write at up to 1480 Mbps, which is their fastest speed. They can easily manage the high transfer rates required for 4K picture shooting because of their consistent write speed of up to 400MB/second. However, as was previously noted, the camera is not able to record a continuous video sequence for more than 29 minutes. However, you may immediately begin filming the following clip, so you will miss around 30 seconds of the action. This obviously indicates that you have ample battery life and memory card capacity.

+ **Make sure to bring extra cards**. You most likely shoot still photos on a regular basis. It's simple to determine how much of your memory card you've used up and how much is remaining since the LCD monitor and viewfinder displays indicate how many shots are left. This is a really unusual method of using videos. The camera displays you how much room is available for a clip while you film, but it could be hard to link that to how much space is left on your memory card. Navigate to the Video Recording menu to see how much space is remaining. It is thus advisable to have many more cards than you anticipate using.

+ **Add a microphone from outside**. To improve sound quality and prevent the sound of the zoom motor or autofocus from being picked up, get an external stereo microphone.

+ **Reduce the amount of zooming**. The ability to fill the frame with a distant topic by zooming in is helpful, but before you do so, consider your options carefully. You will hear the zoom ring spinning when you play a video if you are not using an external microphone. Viewers of your films will find several little zooms to be quite unpleasant. Additionally, digital zoom will result in a lower-quality picture. If quality is more essential than capturing a particular topic, such as a well-known movie star from a distance, digital zoom should not be employed.

+ **Verify that the battery is fully charged**. At typical (non-winter) conditions, a fresh battery will last around 85 minutes of capture time. However, if the emphasis is shifted significantly, this period may be shortened. However, clips are limited to 29 minutes apiece.

- **Keep it calm**. Keep the camera in a cool place since excessive heat may seriously degrade the quality of the video. When photographing outdoors during the summer, the sensor may heat up more quickly than normal. After around five seconds, the camera will cease recording and shut off if there is a risk of overheating. Don't use it again until it has cooled.
- **All you have to do is press the video button**. Holding it down is not necessary. In order to end the recording, press it once more.

Taking Video

In the Video Recording submenu, you have the following choices. The various choices that are available are described in each one. That information will not be duplicated here. Many of them are identical to the still photography elements in the Photo Shooting menu.

- **Naming of the file:** In my opinion, you should use a different character in place of the DSC characters that are used by default in movie file names in Movie mode. I use MOV for video and NZ7/NZ6 for still photos. The guidelines and procedures for this option are the same as those for the Photo Shooting menu's File Naming option.

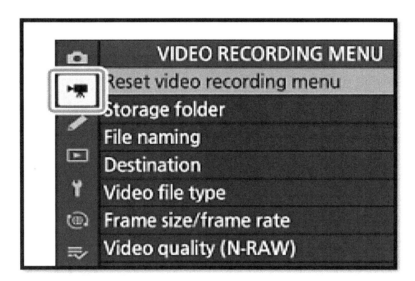

- **The final destination**: It is possible to configure the two memory card slots such that only one is utilized for video storage. The card used for video may be switched from the Photo Shooting menu's Card Type and Secondary Slot

130

Function options. The duration of time you have to save films is shown when you choose a location.

- ⁜ **Picture Area**: This item specifies the visual area utilized for filming movies. You may choose from a number of options:
  - ➤ Select the Image Region. FX and DX are the two choices that allow you to record movies in what Nikon refers to as "FX-based movie format" and "DX-based movie format." The latter creates a 16:9 (HDTV) region out of the full-frame image. In the video industry, DX/APS-C movies are sometimes referred to as APS-C/Super 35 movies; the latter is the most often used term for the video snipping format.

Fortunately, the region that has been taken off is visible without the use of a mask. Instead, it enlarges the captured component to fit in the frame, as shown in the figure's lower right corner. The typical FX-format view appears at the bottom left.

Applying DX Lenses

The camera will automatically transition to a DX-based video format if you use the FTZ adapter to connect a lens that it detects as a DX/APS-C lens. It will make the decision between FX and DX for you; you won't even need to utilize the Choose Image Area box. You can't make the camera utilize the DX lens like it's a full-frame lens, just like in still picture mode. Note that other manufacturers' APS-C (DX) lenses may or may not be recognized by the camera. In order to compensate for camera movement, the camera crops a little when Electronic VR is selected from the i button menu or the Video Recording menu. Slow-motion videos are always cropped.

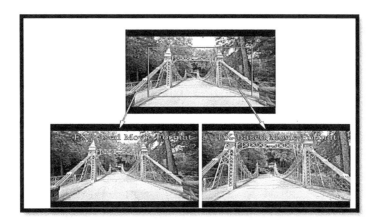

- ⁜ **The size and rate of the frame**: Ten alternative formats are available for standard movies, and three more are available for slow-motion films. The default settings are Full HD at 1920 × 1080 resolution at 60/50/30/25/24 frames per second, Standard HD at 1280 × 720 resolution at 60/50 frames per second, and 4K video at 3840 × 2160 resolution at 30/25/24 frames per second (with 4K 60p with the early 2021 firmware upgrade). As previously stated, PAL television systems in other countries employ 50/25 frames per second, whereas the NTSC system in the US, Japan, and other countries uses the other frame rates.

- **The quality of the video:** You have the option of selecting Normal Quality or High Quality. Your decision affects the duration of the movies you can record, the maximum bit rate that can be maintained, and the sharpness and detail of your picture. If you have fast memory cards and want to display your movie at larger sizes, I suggest High Quality. You can still record 4K video in the High-Quality setting when you choose UHD capture, however the Video Quality option is grayed out. Most movie editing software allows you to switch to a lower-resolution version of a video.

- **The kind of video file:** You may choose between MP4 and MOV formats. Although it is compatible with Windows systems, MOV is the ideal file format for Macintosh devices. However, MP4 is more widely used and compatible with both Macs and PCs. Movie editing software may be switched between them.

- **Video ISO Sensitivity Settings:** For manual exposure mode, you may choose a fixed ISO between 100 and 25600, as well as Hi 0.3, Hi 0.7, Hi 1, and Hi 2. This option allows you to accomplish that, much like the ISO settings in the Photo Shooting menu. You have better control over the ISO that is utilized as a result. When recording movies in P, A, or S exposure settings, the Auto ISO sensitivity is always used. If you want to use it in manual exposure mode, you may switch Auto ISO on or off here. Additionally, you have the option to choose the highest ISO that will be selected automatically, ranging from ISO 64 to Hi 5.0.

- **White Balance**: You may choose the white balance that is utilized while filming.
  - ➢ One option is the same as Photo Settings. The camera will utilize the white balance setting you selected in the Photo Shooting menu.
  - ➢ Choose any of the other options for White Balance. The selection process will only be open to videos. Because it might be difficult to adjust the white balance of video clips, you will usually want to pick Auto white balance or a specified white balance from this menu option. For static images, I usually leave this setting alone.

- **Put Picture Control in place**. You may choose a Picture Control that you will exclusively use while filming videos or you can choose Settings that are the same as photographs. The procedures for selecting and modifying a Picture Control are the same as in this menu item.

One notable feature of the Flat Picture Control, which is available in both picture and video modes, is that it produces a drab, blurry image. Why would you want that? Compared to Standard and the other Picture Control settings, Flat captures a greater dynamic range. This improves the "raw" video picture so you can use your video editing software's color-grading capabilities to make it seem better. Grading allows you to adjust the black level, white point, contrast, color, saturation, and detail. It performs well with images that are somewhat flat, such as those created using N-log gamma or the Flat Picture Control.

- **Manage Picture Control:** Similar to the Photo Shooting menu, this function allows you to load, save, modify, rename, and remove Picture Control settings. You may recover a stored Picture Control from a memory card, make modifications to it, alter its name, delete a style, or duplicate it.
- With Active D-Lighting, you may change the lighting by selecting "Same as Photo Settings," "Extra High," "High," "Normal," "Low," or completely turning it off.
- **High ISO Noise Reduction:** Since long exposure photos are not utilized while recording videos, only High ISO Noise Reduction is accessible in video mode. It may be turned off, low, normal, or high.
- **Lens Corrections:** By addressing lens-specific defects, Vignette Control, Diffraction Compensation, and Auto Distortion Control assist enhance picture quality in the same way they do for still photography.
- **Flicker Reduction:** Depending on your lighting conditions, you may choose Auto, 50Hz, or 60Hz to reduce flickering while recording videos.
- **Metering Modes:** The camera can determine exposure in video mode using Matrix, Center-weighted, and Highlight-weighted metering. However, there is no spot metering accessible.
- **Focus Modes:** AF-S (Single), AF-C (Continuous), Manual Focus, or AF-F (Full-time) are your options. With AF-F permanently engaged in Movie mode, focus is maintained constantly without the need of the shutter or AF-ON button. This guarantees rapid focus changes while recording, despite the fact that it uses more power.
- **AF-Area Modes:** The video mode provides four autofocus settings: auto-area, wide-area (big), wide-area (small), and single-point. For video, pinpoint autofocus is not accessible.
- **Subject Detection in AF/MF:** This function enables the camera to give certain subjects—like people, animals, or objects—priority focus. When you want exact focus control in cluttered environments, it's very helpful.
  - ➢ The camera will attempt to focus even if it is unable to identify the kind of subject you have selected if the AF When Subject Not Detected option is

enabled. This guarantees that even if your primary topic is obscured or absent, something in the frame will remain in focus.

> ➤ The camera won't autofocus if this option is off until it recognizes the designated subject type. This increases your control by keeping the camera from concentrating on backdrops or items that you don't want it to.

+ The built-in stabilization of the camera is controlled via vibration reduction, or VR. "Same as Photo Settings," "On (Normal)," "Sport," or "Off" are the available options.

+ In contrast to in-body image stabilization (IBIS), electronic vibration reduction (VR) counteracts camera motions by making minor cropping and frame changes. Although it is not accessible in Slow-Motion mode or at high frame rates (such as 1920x1080 100/120p), it performs well when stabilizing films. A symbol that looks like a "waving hand" displays on the screen while it is activated. Note, however, that the modest cropping creates a little zoomed-in impression by reducing the field of vision.

+ **Audio Input parameters:** You may modify parameters to guarantee high-quality audio while utilizing an external device for sound.

> ➤ Select the [External Mic] option to attach an external microphone. This ensures precise and clear sound capture by optimizing the audio for microphones.

> ➤ Choose [Line] input for audio mixers or other line-level devices. In order to ensure correct audio processing and prevent distortion, this setting is designed for higher voltage line inputs.

Important Information Regarding Line Input

+ **Always Choose [Line]:** Make sure your camera's [Line] option is off if you're connecting an audio device using a line connection. Accidentally selecting [External mic] might result in improper handling of the audio input, which could cause errors when recording. The camera is prepared to handle the various characteristics of line-level audio inputs when the [Line] option is set to true.

+ **Voltage Configuration:** Make sure the audio input voltage is +6 dBV or below if you're using a line to connect audio devices. Line inputs are capable of handling larger voltages than microphone inputs, although going beyond +6 dBV might cause audio distortion and reduce the quality of the recording. The integrity and clarity of the audio signal are preserved when the voltage is kept below this threshold.

Whether you're utilizing a line input or an external microphone, you can be certain that the sound you attach to your camera via an external device is captured accurately and clearly by following these guidelines. By doing this, you may steer clear of technical issues and ensure that your recordings have the highest possible sound quality.

Attenuator: When recording in noisy situations, this option helps lessen audio distortion brought on by loud background noise. In difficult circumstances, turning it on guarantees crisper sound.

Response in Frequency

- **Wide Range:** This option is perfect for capturing a variety of audio in different contexts since it allows you to record a wide range of sounds.
- **Vocal Range:** Select this option if recording vocals is your main goal since it improves the richness and clarity of speaking or singing.
- **Minimize Wind Noise:** Audio quality may be negatively impacted by wind blowing into your microphone. When using the built-in microphones on the camera, this function reduces wind noise. Use it sparingly however, since it may alter other aspects of sound. Look for an integrated wind noise reduction switch on external microphones, such as the Nikon ME-1, and utilize it as necessary.
- **Headphone loudness:** The default setting is 15; however you may adjust the loudness anywhere from 1 to 30. This enables you to keep an eye on your audio levels while recording and modify them as needed.
- **Timecodes:** Providing accurate markers in hours, minutes, seconds, and frames, timecodes are an advanced tool for synchronizing audio and video. This is especially helpful for post-production frame alignment and sophisticated video editing.
  - ➢ The modest variations in actual frame rates are somewhat offset by timecodes (e.g., 30 fps is officially 29.97 fps, while 24 fps is actually 23.976 fps). To guarantee that the frame count precisely corresponds to real-time durations, the system incorporates "drop frame" capability. Although this function is quite helpful, utilizing it calls for a deeper understanding of video editing software, which is beyond the purview of this instruction.

Plug-in Power for the Mic Jack

- ➢ When [OFF] is selected, the camera does not use the microphone jack to power external microphones.
- ➢ When utilizing microphones that don't need power from the camera, it's better to turn the plug-in power [OFF]. By doing this, interference that might decrease audio quality is avoided.
- ➢ To make sure your microphone is compatible with the selected format, always refer to the manufacturer's requirements.

> Enabling plug-in power won't impact an external microphone if you've chosen [Line] under Audio Input in the video menu since the camera doesn't provide power in this mode.

+ **HDMI-based external recording control:** To allow the camera to manage recording on an external recorder, turn this option [ON]. When utilizing an external setup, this streamlines your workflow by enabling you to start and stop recording straight from the camera's controls.

+ **Hi-Res Zoom:** This feature allows you to enlarge your subject without compromising the quality of your images. You may utilize this function without a zoom lens, and it's particularly helpful for close-ups.

Taking your Video

You are now prepared to begin filming.

To film your movies, you must follow these steps:

+ **Connect the microphone:** Attach an external mono or stereo microphone to the left-hand microphone port of the camera using a 3.5mm stereo small connection.

+ **Decide on an exposure setting:** In Program, Shutter Priority, or Aperture Priority, you may manually adjust the exposure. The camera employs matrix metering, which determines exposure based on sensor data.

+ **Modify the Exposure:** The exposure mode you choose will determine what adjustments you may make.

> **The priority of the program or shutter:** Only by adjusting the main command dial and pushing the EV button on top of the camera can you alter the exposure correction. As you make adjustments, the picture on the screen will get darker and brighter. The camera automatically selects the ISO sensitivity and shutter speed.

> **Establish the priority of the aperture:** The exposure compensation may be adjusted using the main command dial and the EV button, while the f/stop can be adjusted using the sub-command dial. The camera automatically selects the ISO sensitivity and shutter speed.

> **Exposure by hand:** The shutter speed, which may be adjusted between 1/25th and 1/4000th second, is controlled by the primary command dial, while the aperture is controlled by the secondary one. Holding down the ISO button while rotating the main command dial allows you to adjust the ISO sensitivity.

+ **Turn on video capture:** Turn the Photo/Movie switch to the Movie position to begin recording a movie.

136

- **Choose an Area Mode for Focus and AF:** You can choose between autofocus and manual focus using the AF/MF switch on the camera body. Next, choose the AF-area mode by selecting either AF-S or AF-F.
- **Adjust the sound level:** To choose the recording's volume level, select the Microphone Sensitivity option from the Video Recording menu. After that, you may choose Manual Sensitivity to adjust the level using an audiometer or Auto Sensitivity to let the camera to do it. If you wish to use video editing software to add music, a voice-over track, or other sounds after the fact, you may also record a silent film without sound.
- **Turn on and off the recording:** To begin filming and lock in focus, press the button with the red dots. To stop the recording, press the button once more. When you record video, the LCD display monitor looks like the picture below. Although it is arranged somewhat differently and does not obscure the picture area, the information on the viewfinder display is same. You may adjust the amount of information that appears on top of the video by hitting the DISP button while the video is being recorded.
- **No flash:** You can use the Nikon SB-500's integrated LED movie light when filming, but you can't use an electric flash.

Making use of the i Button

The "i" button, which is crucial in Photo mode, allows you to adjust parameters and settings in real time while filming. Professional videographers will be acquainted with and appreciate some special equipment that still photographers may not be. You may use them to improve your films while you're shooting them.

- **Picture Control:** You may alter the colors, contrast, and sharpness of your films by selecting from a variety of Picture Control options.
- **Frame Size/Rate and Image Quality:** Choose the frame rate and image quality that you like most. Depending on your requirements—such as more detail or lesser file sizes—you may choose between High and Normal quality.
- **Select the Image region:** Choose the region where movies will be recorded. This gives you control over the sensor's use.
- **Wi-Fi Connectivity:** Use this to control the Wi-Fi settings on your camera. The connection may be turned on or off, or it can be used for other purposes like file transfers or remote control.
- **Electronic VR (Vibration Reduction):** To steady your movies, turn Electronic VR on or off. This is particularly useful for minimizing shakiness while shooting handheld.
- **AF-Area option:** Select the autofocus option that best fits your video needs. During recording, you may adjust how the camera focuses on your subjects with the use of these settings.
- **Adjust White Balance:** Make sure your films' white balance is in line with the lighting. Accurate color reproduction is ensured by proper white balance.
- **Microphone Sensitivity:** During recording, change the microphone's sensitivity. Both the external and built-in stereo microphones are impacted by this. For example, you may reduce unwanted noise by lowering the microphone's sensitivity if a loud noise, such as a jackhammer, begins to play nearby. On the other hand, sensitivity is raised in quieter settings to record more sound information.

- ✦ **Metering Mode:** To regulate how the camera assesses light for video exposure, choose from Matrix, Center-weighted, or Highlight-weighted metering modes. Keep in mind that Movie mode does not support Spot metering.
- ✦ **View Memory Card Information:** This function displays the settings that are currently in place for your memory card slots, including RAW Primary-JPEG Secondary, Backup, and Overflow. Although you have to utilize the Photo Shooting menu to make adjustments, you may check these options here.
- ✦ Reduce vibration by turning on or off in-body image stabilization (IBIS). Smoother videos are guaranteed by this function, which lessens camera wobble, particularly when recording handheld.
- ✦ **Focus setting:** Choose the focus setting that best suits your requirements while recording:

> o **AF-S (Single AF):** For stationary subjects.
> o **AF-C (Continuous AF):** For moving subjects.
> o **AF-F (Full-time AF):** Focus remains active continuously without pressing the shutter button.
> o **Manual Focus:** Manually control focus for precise adjustments.

You may believe that your camera's video frames would be sharper if you increase the shutter speed. However, choosing the ideal shutter speed for video is a bit more difficult. First, regardless of the exposure option you choose (Auto, P, S, or A), you are unable to alter the shutter speed of your movies. You may choose a shutter speed when you go to manual exposure. It operates like this.

- ✦ **Priority modes for programs and shutters:** The camera uses the illumination to determine the ISO sensitivity and shutter speed (such as 1/30th of a second). Pressing the EV button to add or remove exposure compensation is your sole exposure compensation option. As one may think, if you want to photograph creatively, P and S settings are not the greatest choice.
- ✦ **Aperture-Priority Mode should be used:** You may set an aperture in this mode that will allow you to employ selective focus with varying depth of field. You may choose any f/stop that is compatible with your lens while in A mode, and the camera will automatically determine the ideal shutter speed and ISO level. The camera will often reduce the ISO sensitivity as much as possible to maintain the shutter speed at 1/30th second when you choose a big aperture. Then, it will choose slower shutter speeds if strong illumination is required. When I attempt to photograph outdoors in direct sunshine at f/1.8 or f/1.4, my camera goes to the 1/200th second. You may adjust the exposure even in A mode.

ᐩ Manual Exposure Mode should be used. In this mode, you may still adjust the ISO, shutter speed (from 1/25th second to 1/8000th second), and aperture even if your settings produce entirely dark or washed-out video. Since video capture might vary from 24 to 60 frames per second, you cannot choose a shutter speed that is quicker than the frame rate. If your video setting is 1920 × 1080 at 30 frames per second, you cannot choose a shutter speed quicker than 1/30th second.

Exposure via Semi-Manual

The ISO Sensitivity Settings option in the Video Recording menu activates Auto ISO Control (Mode M). When engaged, the camera will try to adjust the ISO setting to provide the optimal exposure based on the shutter speed, aperture, and exposure compensation settings that are currently in place. If you choose a suitable shutter speed (as suggested below) and an f/stop in manual exposure mode, the camera will effectively expose the subject. So, how does one choose the ideal shutter speed? As you may expect, the ideal course of action is to adjust the exposure by varying the aperture and/or ISO sensitivity while maintaining the shutter speed at 1/30th second. We don't notice whether our subjects are fuzzy because they are moving since we don't gaze at a video frame for more than 1/30th or 1/24th of a second. Although camera shaking might be annoying, virtual reality often resolves this issue. Because each frame passes by so rapidly, the shutter speed of 1/30th second is much better for video than still photography. It might be challenging to get quality images with a quicker shutter speed. Only about 12% of the 1/30th second that had elapsed is really caught when you shoot a video frame with a shutter speed of 1/200th second. However, one frame takes up 1/30th of a second when it is played back, and 88% of that time is spent enlarging the original picture to fit the frame. This often results in a picture that is overly sharp and choppy or jumpy. Hollywood films that were filmed using shutter speeds half the reciprocal of the bespoke frame rate are what we all grew up viewing. This is not so much a scientific explanation as a societal one. A movie camera requires a 180-degree shutter "angle" for a 1/48-second exposure, but the impact on our perception of what we see is the same. For the most "film-like" look, use a shutter speed of 1/60th second and 24 frames per second. Faster shutter speeds are helpful for several motion analysis applications, particularly when examining single frames. 1/30th or 1/60th of a second will usually work. Reduce the ISO or use a neutral-density filter to reduce the amount of light entering the lens for the ideal exposure. You may utilize a quicker shutter speed as a result. Using 1/60th second or slower at 24 frames per second, 1/60th second or slower at 30 frames per second, and 1/126th second or slower at 60 frames per second is a decent guideline for recording progressive video (as opposed to interlaced video, which the camera cannot handle).

Viewing Your Videos

Your films are prepared for viewing after you have finished recording them. When you look at still images, you see film clips, but they are distinct because they have a "Play" button and a movie camera symbol on top of them. Playback is initiated by pressing the multi-selector's center button.

During playback, you may perform the following:

- **Stop Playback:** Use the multi-selector's down button to stop a video clip while it's playing. Press the multi-selector's center button to start playing again.
- **Rewind and Fast Forward:** To rewind or move through the footage, use the multi-selector left and right buttons. For 2x speed, press once; for 8x speed, press twice; and for 16x speed, press three times. Holding down the corresponding button will take you to the start or finish of the footage.
- **Begin Slow-Motion Playback:** Press the down button to begin playing a stopped video clip in slow motion.
- **Skip 10 Seconds:** During playback, use the main command dial to forward or rewind by 10 seconds.
- **Jump to Index Markers:** To go to the previous or next index marker, turn the sub-command dial. The dial will advance to the clip's beginning or final frame if no markers are selected. A "paddle" indicator at the top of the screen denotes indexed areas while an indexed movie is playing.
- **Modify Volume:** During playback, use the Zoom In button to raise the volume and the Zoom Out button to decrease it.
- **Trim Video and Save Frames:** To access choices for either storing individual frames or trimming the video, use the i button. To make changes, adhere to the on-screen instructions.
- **End Playback:** Press the Playback button or the multi-selector's up button to end playback and go back to the main screen.
- **Return to Shooting Mode:** Press the Movie button to return to shooting mode after stopping playback.
- **Access Menus:** After stopping the video, click the MENU button to see or modify camera menus.

Taking your movies and trimming them

When editing a clip on the camera, you can only trim the start and finish of a clip that is at least two seconds long. You will need a software that can deal with AVI video clips if you want to conduct more comprehensive editing. You may search for "AVI Editor" to locate any of the hundreds of free video editors available online, or you can use a premium application like Corel Video Studio, Adobe Premiere Elements, or Pinnacle Studio. These will enable you to add titles, special effects, and scene changes to a movie that is composed of many segments. You may edit or cut footage in the camera while it's playing or via the Retouch menu. **The process remains unchanged. You may learn how to edit or chop video in-camera by following these steps:**

+ **Play the video clip:** Press the multi-selector center button to begin playing of the clip you want to modify. To see the photographs, click the Playback button. The music will start. Next, follow its instructions, beginning with Step 2. Another option is to locate the clip you want to edit in the Retouch menu. Next, choose the option to Change Video.

+ **Switch on the editing feature:** Press the down button to remove the video from the start after pausing a movie at the first frame you want to save. The current point of the film will be shown in the movie progress bar located in the lower left corner of the screen. You may switch between frames while the movie is paused by using the main or sub-command knobs, or the left and right buttons.

+ **Make a trim move**: Press the down button to stop the video once you've seen it through to the last frame you want to save. This will enable you to remove footage from the film's conclusion. The next stored index point in the clip may be accessed by turning the main command dial.

+ **Select a beginning and ending point**: To access the movie editing tools in a stopped video, hit the "i" button. After that, choose "Start/End Point." The topic of whether the present frame should be the starting point or the finishing point will be raised. After making your choice, click OK again.

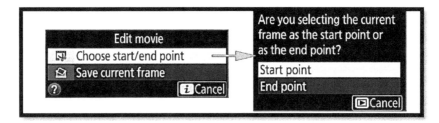

+ **Start the replay again**: Playback may be started or stopped using the multi-selector center button. The main monitor control dial, which takes you to the next saved index point (see figure below), and the Single frame, Pause, Rewind, and Advance displays allow you to navigate about your clip. Keep in mind that your video must be at least two seconds length before you clip it.

142

- **Examine the trim:** Can we proceed? Prompt appears. After selecting "Yes" or "No," click "OK."
- **Store the video:** There are four ways to store the shortened film:
  - ➢ **Save the file as a new one:** The original film will be preserved, but the trimmed clip will be stored as a new file.
  - ➢ **Replace the current file:** The original movie on your memory card is replaced with the trimmed clip. Because you won't be able to get your unedited footage back, use this option carefully.
  - ➢ **Cancel**: Go back to editing mode.
  - ➢ **A sneak peek:** Check out the revised version. After that, you have the option to cancel, overwrite, or save it as a new file.

The camera will show a green progress bar and a Saving Movie message while it stores the trimmed clip on your memory card. You don't want to tamper with it or lose the clip you've saved since storing anything takes time. Make sure your camera's battery is completely charged before you begin editing footage.

Storing a Frame

Any frame of your movie that matches the resolution of your video format may be readily saved as a JPEG still. **Here's how to do it:**

- **Pause at the Frame:** To pause your movie at the frame you want to preserve, use the down button.
- Select Save Selected Frame from the menu by pressing the i button to access the Save Option.
- **Save the Frame:** To make a still copy of the stopped frame, use the up button.
- **Confirm Save:** To complete and save the frame, choose Proceed and hit OK.
- **File Location:** A JPEG picture of the saved frame will be kept on your memory card.

This technique is fast and guarantees that you may extract certain moments from your films without the need for further software.

CHAPTER SIX
ABOUT ADD-ONS AND ACCESSORIES

Selecting Appropriate Lenses for Every Circumstance

Wide-aperture prime lenses for portrait photography

You want a lens for portrait photography that blurs out the backdrop and brings your subject into clear focus. Shallow depth of field, as it is called, is crucial for separating your subject from distracting objects.

Suggested Lens

+ The Nikon Z 50mm f/1.8 S is an excellent choice for taking portraits. The f/1.8 aperture produces bokeh, or a gorgeously blurred backdrop, which highlights your subject. Even at the widest aperture, its clarity and sharpness are superb.
+ Photographer Nikon Z 85mm f/1.8 S Another great option for portraiture is the 85mm f/1.8, which has a slightly larger focal length. It lets you photograph from a larger distance and gives you even more backdrop compression, which may make your subject seem more attractive.

What Makes These Lenses the Best?

+ **Wide Aperture:** You can photograph in low light and get that creamy, fuzzy backdrop with the f/1.8 aperture.
+ **Focal Length:** 50mm to 85mm is the usual range for portrait lenses. With these focus lengths; you may create beautiful proportions while keeping a comfortable distance from your subject.

Wide-Angle Lenses for Photographing Landscapes

A lens with a large field of view and excellent foreground-to-background sharpness is usually required for landscape photography. Capturing the expanse of nature, cityscapes, or enormous architectural buildings requires the use of a wide-angle lens.

Suggested Lens

+ A wide-angle zoom lens, the Nikon Z 14-30mm f/4 S has a flexible focal length range of 14mm (ultra wide) to 30mm (still wide but less extreme). The lens produces crisp pictures across the frame, and the f/4 aperture is wide enough for the majority of daytime circumstances.

- The Nikon Z 24mm f/1.8 S is a great alternative for landscape photographers who like prime lenses since it offers a little broader perspective and better low-light performance than the zoom.

What Makes These Lenses the Best?

- **Wide Field of View:** More of the scene may be captured in a single picture when using a wide-angle lens.
- **Clarity and Sharpness:** These lenses work best at lower apertures like f/8 or f/16 since you want sharp details throughout the picture while taking landscape photos.
- **Weather Sealing:** A lot of landscape photographers work in inclement weather. Weather sealing on the 14-30mm f/4 S helps keep your equipment safe.

Telephoto Lenses for Photographing Wildlife

A lens that enables you to get close-ups of animals from a distance is often necessary for wildlife photography. You can zoom in on subjects with a telephoto lens without upsetting them. By producing crisp, well-defined objects with a pleasingly blurred backdrop, these lenses also enable you to separate animals from its environment.

Suggested Lens

- This is a professional-grade telephoto zoom lens: Nikon Z 70-200mm f/2.8 VR S. You can photograph a wide range of things at various distances, including birds in flight and animals in the wild, thanks to the 70-200mm focal range. You have better control over the background blur (bokeh) and excellent performance in low light because to the f/2.8 aperture.
- Nikon Z f/4.5-5.6 VR S 100-400mm With its 100-400mm focal range, this super-telephoto zoom lens lets you get even closer to far-off animals. When shooting at long focal lengths, the VR (Vibration Reduction) helps minimize blur caused by camera shaking.

What Makes These Lenses the Best?

- **Telephoto Focal Length:** You may take pictures of animals without disturbing them by using a telephoto lens.

- **Fast Aperture (f/2.8):** Make your subject stand out against a fuzzy backdrop by using a fast aperture to photograph in low light while keeping a shallow depth of focus.
- **Vibration Reduction:** VR is crucial for guaranteeing clear shots at longer focal lengths since telephoto lenses may amplify camera shaking.

For Street Photography: Small and Quick Cameras

Capturing impromptu moments in dynamic settings is a common task for street photographers. This calls for a small, quick lens that you can take about and use in a variety of lighting situations.

Suggested Lens

- The Nikon Z 35mm f/1.8 S is an excellent lens for street photography. Excellent low-light performance is provided by the f/1.8 aperture, and the 35mm focal length is sufficiently broad to capture the surroundings while maintaining subject focus. Additionally, it is lightweight and small, which makes it ideal for street use.
- **Nikon Z 50mm f/1.8 S:** This is an excellent choice if you would like a slightly larger focal length. It provides greater compression, which makes it a suitable option for more personal photographs or portraits, but it's still broad enough for the majority of street scenes.

What Makes These Lenses the Best?

- **Compact Size:** These lenses are ideal for candid photography because of their compact size and lack of noticeable presence.
- **Fast Aperture:** The wide f/1.8 aperture helps separate objects from the backdrop and improves low-light performance.
- **Versatility:** A 35mm or 50mm lens may be used for a variety of street photography techniques, such as close-up, more personal portraiture and expansive environmental photos.

Specific Macro Lenses for Macro Photographic Applications

You may take very close-up pictures of little objects, such as insects, flowers, or textures, using macro photography. To do this, you'll need a macro lens that has a high magnification, crisp detail, and the ability to focus at extremely close range.

Suggested Lens

- **Nikon Z 105mm f/2.8 VR S Macro:** This lens is ideal for taking thorough close-ups of tiny objects. Because of its 1:1 magnification ratio, you may photograph your subject at its true size. Beautiful background blur is possible with the f/2.8 aperture, and even at extremely close range, the Vibration Reduction (VR) helps maintain stable photos.
- **Nikon Z 50mm f/2.8 Macro:** This camera provides a smaller form factor and yet has good macro capabilities if you're searching for a more portable solution.

What Makes These Lenses the Best?

- **1:1 Magnification:** You may photograph subjects at life-size magnification by using macro lenses.
- **Sharpness:** Even at very close ranges, macro lenses are designed to provide the highest clarity and fine detail.
- **Image Stabilization:** VR helps minimize camera shaking since macro photography often entails handheld shooting at close range.

Zoom Lenses for All-Rounder Travel Photography

Because you can be photographing street scenes, architecture, landscapes, portraits, and more, travel photography demands adaptability. To avoid having to change lenses all the time, you'll need a lens that can tolerate a range of conditions.

Suggested Lens

- **Nikon Z 24-70mm f/4 S:** This lens is an excellent travel all-arounder. It includes short telephoto (70mm) pictures for detail and portraits and wide-angle (24mm) shots for landscapes. For the majority of travel situations, the f/4 aperture is appropriate, and the small size makes it portable.
- Nikon Z f/3.5-6.3 VR 18-140mm With its broader focal range, the 18-140mm gives you even more versatility, enabling you to use a single lens to record both wide-angle and telephoto subjects. It's perfect for taking pictures of a broad range of things while on the run.

What Makes These Lenses the Best?

- **Versatility:** You may capture a variety of focus lengths with a zoom lens, including architecture, portraits, and landscapes.

- **Lightweight and compact:** lightweight lenses that are ideal for travel.
- **Image Stabilization:** This is useful for handheld photography, particularly at longer lens lengths.

Top Performance Memory Cards

For your Nikon Z50 II to operate flawlessly, selecting the right memory card is essential, particularly when taking high-resolution pictures or recording 4K video. Performance, reliability, and data transfer rates may all be greatly enhanced with the right memory card. Knowing the different memory card choices and how they impact your shooting experience is essential since the Nikon Z50 II supports both UHS-I and UHS-II SD cards.

Extreme Pro SD UHS-II SanDisk (V90)

One of the greatest choices for photographers and videographers looking for the highest performance is the SanDisk Extreme Pro SD UHS-II. This high-end card is renowned for its quick read and writes speeds, which are necessary for high-resolution video recording, continuous shooting modes, and quick shooting.

- With a read speed of up to 300 MB/s and a write speed of up to 260 MB/s, the SanDisk Extreme Pro card can quickly write large amounts of data, such as RAW images and 4K video. Because of this, it works well in fast-paced shooting scenarios when every second counts.
- **Durability:** The memory card is designed to withstand harsh conditions. It is very reliable in a range of shooting situations since it is X-ray, shock, temperature, and moisture resistant.Professional photographers and videographers that use 4K and high-speed burst modes will love this card.

The V90 Lexar Professional 2000X SD UHS-II

Another great choice for high-performance photography and video creation is the Lexar Professional 2000x SD UHS-II card, which boasts remarkable transfer rates that aid to expedite the process, particularly when dealing with large picture files and 4K video.

- The Lexar 2000x card can read and write data at up to 300 MB/s and 260 MB/s, respectively, much as the SanDisk Extreme Pro. It has no trouble handling 4K footage and fast filming.
- **Durability:** Similar to the SanDisk high Pro, the Lexar 2000x is resistant to shock, water, and extreme temperatures. It's a reliable choice for those who shoot in unpredictable situations.Photographers and filmmakers who need speed and reliability—particularly in hectic or demanding shooting scenarios—are the greatest candidates for this card.

Sony SF-G Tough Series UHS-II SD Cards (V90)

The Sony SF-G Tough Series SD card is ideal for the Nikon Z50 II since it is designed for excellent performance. It is particularly appropriate for those who seek a memory card that is both fast and durable.

- With read and write speeds of up to 300 MB/s and 299 MB/s, respectively, the Sony SF-G Tough card allows for quick data transfer for 4K video and high-resolution images.
- **Durability:** This memory card is perfect for outdoor or adventure photography since it is strong and fast, and it is resistant to shock, water, and dust. It can also tolerate extreme temperatures, making it a great option for challenging conditions.

The Kingston Canvas React plus UHS-II (V90)

Another excellent choice for Nikon Z50 II users is Kingston's Canvas React Plus, which offers exceptional speed and performance at a lesser cost than some of the other high-end cards.

- The card is perfect for photo and video applications since it has rapid read and write speeds of up to 300 MB/s and 260 MB/s. It is fast enough to process large RAW files, 4K video, and burst shots.
- **Durability:** This card is impervious to X-rays, shock, and water. For photographers looking for a reliable card for outdoor and vacation photos, it's a great option.
- For those looking for excellent performance at a reasonable cost, the Kingston Canvas React Plus is the best option. For photographers and videographers who want to capture high-quality film without going over budget, it's perfect.

Transcend SDXC UHS-II U3 (V90)

The SDXC UHS-II U3 card is a powerful substitute for owners of the Nikon Z50 II, and Transcend is a well-known name in the memory card market. Compared to other pricey solutions, it offers constant performance and fast speed at a reduced cost.

- With read and write speeds of up to 285 MB/s and 180 MB/s, respectively, the Transcend SDXC UHS-II card is perfect for 4K video recording and continuous shooting. For most users, it offers respectable performance even if it is slower than high-end alternatives like the SanDisk Extreme Pro.
- **Durability:** This card can withstand extreme temperatures, shock, and water, making it appropriate for a range of shooting conditions.

- For photographers and videographers who want reliable performance without shelling out a lot of cash for the fastest cards, the Transcend SDXC UHS-II is a great choice. It is particularly appropriate for semi-professionals and amateurs.

PNY SDXC UHS-I U3 Elite Performance (V30)

The PNY Elite Performance SDXC UHS-I U3 card is a great option for customers on a low budget who don't need UHS-II speeds. Despite not having UHS-II cards' high-speed capabilities, it nevertheless works well for standard photography and video recording.

- The PNY Elite Performance can read and write data at up to 100 MB/s and 90 MB/s, respectively. Even while these speeds aren't as quick as UHS-II cards, they are still enough for 1080p video and burst shooting at slower frame rates.
- **Durability:** The PNY Elite Performance card is perfect for entry-level photographers or those who don't want 4K video but still need solid memory for everyday photography since it is shockproof, waterproof, and temperature-resistant, making it appropriate for daily use.

Selecting the Best Memory Card

There are many factors to take into account when choosing a memory card for your Nikon Z50 II:

- A card with rapid read and write speeds is necessary for optimal performance while recording 4K video or continuous burst pictures. While UHS-I cards may still fulfill standard photography criteria, UHS-II cards are faster and more effective for certain tasks.
- SD cards up to 1TB in capacity may be used with the Nikon Z50 II. For lengthier sessions, you may want a card with a greater capacity, depending on your shooting style, particularly if you're shooting RAW or 4K video.
- Select a card that can withstand temperature changes, stress, and water if you shoot outside or in challenging conditions on a regular basis.
- Although they cost more, high-end UHS-II cards perform better. There are other UHS-I cards that provide respectable performance at a reduced price if you don't need the quickest speeds.

External Microphones to Enhance Sound Quality

Rode VideoMicro: Small and Inexpensive

The Rode VideoMicro is a great choice for beginners or those on a limited budget seeking a straightforward plug-and-play solution. This small, light microphone connects via a 3.5mm connector and inserts into the camera's hot shoe. The simplicity of the VideoMicro—it draws power directly from the camera, without the need for an external power source—is one of its key advantages. It is good for general vlogging, interviews, and recording focused audio in less-than-ideal places because of its directional design, which helps to eliminate background noise from the sides and rear. Even though it's not the most powerful microphone, it's perfect for beginners since it strikes a balance between price and quality.

Shure VP83 LensHopper: Sound Quality at the Professional Level

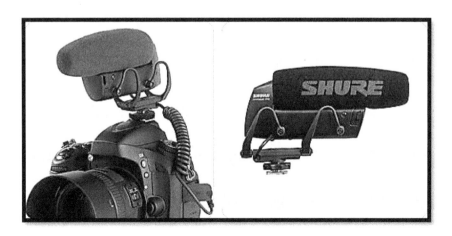

For those who want to enhance their audio quality, the Shure VP83 LensHopper provides more control and performance. The VP83 is more directed and superior at isolating sound from directly in front of the camera due to its supercardioid pickup pattern, which sets it apart from the Rode VideoMicro. This makes it an excellent option for photography in noisy or crowded settings when you need to reject unwanted background noise and direct the microphone's attention to your subject. The Shure VP83 has a robust, high-end construction and runs on an AA battery. This microphone will be very helpful to serious vloggers, YouTubers, and documentary makers that seek reliable audio for high-quality film. It functions well even during outside shooting since its purpose is to lessen wind noise. It is ideal for prolonged use and professional work due to its longer battery life and extensive sound control features.

Rode VideoMic Pro+: Multipurpose and Potent

For those who want the best performance, the Rode VideoMic Pro+ is a high-end shotgun microphone with remarkable sound quality and cutting-edge features. The VideoMic Pro+ boasts excellent sound quality and is thus appropriate for more professional video production, while being more costly than comparable entry-level microphones. Even with background noise, your music will remain clear and sharp because to its highly focused super cardioid polar pattern. The VideoMic Pro+ is notable for its high-frequency boost and high-pass filter settings, which let you customize the audio quality to meet your specific needs. You have greater control over the final product whether you're recording talk, interviews, or ambient sounds. It uses a rechargeable lithium-ion battery, and while not in use, the automatic power-on/off feature helps to save battery life. For producers looking for a more polished solution that blends portability and excellent audio, the VideoMic Pro+ is perfect. This will not let you down if you require a reliable microphone for film projects or shoot a lot of outside footage.

The Sennheiser MKE 400: Small and Adaptable

For those who want high-quality audio but want something smaller than the Rode VideoMic Pro+, the Sennheiser MKE 400 is a great option. It is a hyper cardioid shotgun microphone that rejects noise from the rear and sides while picking up sound from the front. It's a great choice for content creators seeking a little microphone that can be used for a variety of purposes, such as interviews or street vlogs. The MKE 400 is perfect for shooting outdoors or in windy conditions since it has a built-in windshield. It runs on a single AAA battery, much like the majority of microphones in its class, and has an automatic power-off feature to save battery life. Because of its great portability, this microphone is a great choice for YouTubers and vloggers who are always on the go. Its lightweight construction ensures that you won't be burdened throughout shots while yet getting high-quality, reliable audio.

Selecting the Best Microphone for Your Requirements

Take into account the following elements when selecting the ideal external microphone for your Nikon Z50 II:

- **Audio Quality:** Select a microphone that produces crisp, clean sound, particularly for recording interviews or conversation. This is where shotgun microphones, like the Rode VideoMic Pro+ and Shure VP83, shine because of their highly directed pickup patterns, which concentrate on sound in front of the camera.
- **Portability and Size:** Select a small, lightweight microphone, like the Rode VideoMicro or Sennheiser MKE 400, for travel or handheld photography. They are portable and won't significantly increase the weight of your setup.
- **Cost:** Professional producers who need high-quality audio may use the Shure VP83 and Rode VideoMic Pro+, while others, like the Rode VideoMicro and Sennheiser MKE 400, are more reasonably priced. Make a decision based on your budget and personal needs.

- **Source of Power:** Certain microphones, including the Sennheiser MKE 400 and Shure VP83, need their own batteries. Others get power directly from the camera, such as the Rode VideoMicro. If you wish to photograph for a long time, think about the convenience of battery life and the need for recharging choices.

Gimbals, Filters, and Additional Accessories

Using your Nikon Z50 II to take excellent pictures and videos involves more than simply using the camera itself. Whether you're vlogging, creating dramatic images, or filming in a range of lighting conditions, adding the right accessories may significantly improve your content. The technical and artistic aspects of your shots may be greatly enhanced by these accessories, which include gimbals to stabilize your footage and filters to assist adjust light and color. We'll examine some of the best add-ons for enhancing your Nikon Z50 II setup below.

Filters: Improving Control of Light and Color

For both photographers and filmmakers, filters are an essential tool. They serve a variety of purposes, from enhancing contrast and saturation to reducing glare and reflections. You can get the finest photo with the Nikon Z50 II by using certain filters, particularly in challenging lighting conditions. **Here are a few of the most well-liked and useful filters to think about:**
- **UV Filters:** Adding a UV filter may protect the lens even if the Nikon Z50 II sensor is protected. In addition to helping shield the front element of your lens from dust, scratches, and minor impacts, UV filters are primarily designed to prevent ultraviolet light. Although UV radiation have less of an effect on digital sensors, adding this filter to your lens helps to preserve its quality and provides you piece of mind.
- **Filters with Neutral Density (ND):** helpful for obtaining perfect depth of focus with wide apertures or for filming in bright environments. In essence, it reduces the amount of light that reaches the camera, enabling you to use wider apertures or slower shutter speeds without overexposing your photos. For filmmakers hoping to create a fluid motion blur in their films, this is crucial.
- Polarizing filters are helpful for lowering haze, glare, and reflections in nature or outdoor photography. These filters aid in increasing contrast, reducing reflections from glass or water, and saturating colors. For landscape photography, they are particularly helpful since they guarantee a rich blue sky and make your subject stand out against a vibrant backdrop.

Variable ND Filters: These filters have more adjustability than ND filters while still providing the same advantages. A variable ND filter gives you total control over exposure without requiring you to adjust any camera settings since you can spin the filter to change the amount of light reduction. For filmmakers who need to adjust exposure while on the fly, especially during a session with a range of lighting conditions, it's fantastic.

Gimbals: Providing Stability for Smooth Video

A gimbal is one of the most essential tools for video producers looking to enhance the quality of their pictures. Even though the Nikon Z50 II is a lightweight mirrorless camera, handheld video may sometimes produce shaky pictures, especially when moving or using lower shutter speeds. By stabilizing the camera, a gimbal enables you to record fluid, dramatic shots while running, walking, or otherwise moving.

 For mirrorless cameras such as the Z50 II, the DJI Ronin-SC is a portable gimbal that offers three-axis stabilization for steady images. It is little and simple to use. Even in dynamic shooting situations, it can produce perfect film because to its high payload capacity, which can hold a variety of lenses and accessories. Additionally, the Ronin-SC includes many clever features, such as Time-lapse and ActiveTrack, which make it perfect for artistic images.

 For the Nikon Z50 II, the Zhiyun Crane 2S gimbal is a dependable and sturdy choice. It can accommodate bulky camera setups and add-ons. The Crane 2S is renowned for its robust construction and seamless operation, which produce professional-caliber footage with little effort. Additionally, it has a follow-focus wheel that facilitates focus switching when shooting.

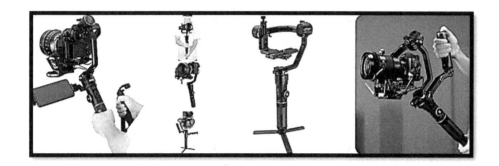

- The highly regarded Moza AirCross 2 gimbal is capable of supporting mirrorless cameras such as the Z50 II with ease. Its lightweight form provides excellent stabilizing capabilities. The Moza AirCross 2 is perfect for extended shooting sessions because of its long battery life and user-friendly control system, which produces dependable still and video footage. The gimbal has a number of shooting options, including as Pan Follow, Lock, and Inception Mode, for more creative flexibility.

Whether you're walking, running, or shooting action scenes, using a gimbal with your Nikon Z50 II will provide fluid and dramatic footage. Additionally, the enhanced stability allows you to use slower shutter speeds in films to get a more realistic motion blur, which gives them a polished look.

Additional accessories to Enhance Your Setup

There are a number of other accessories that might enhance your Nikon Z50 II shooting experience in addition to filters and gimbals.

- **External Flash or Lighting:** For improved control and power, it is advised to utilize an external flash or continuous lighting system, even if the Z50 II has a built-in flash. Your videos and photos may be greatly impacted by lighting, particularly in low light. For portraits or commercial photos, a softbox or ring light may aid to diffuse shadows and provide uniform lighting. An external LED light panel may help you control exposure and provide a polished look to your scenes while you're filming.

- **Tripods:** When arranging time-lapses or long exposure photographs, a sturdy tripod is essential for hands-free photography. Look for tripods with a smooth pan-and-tilt head, flexible legs, and height adjustment to aid with video production. Additionally, some tripods include fluid heads designed specifically for videos, which enable more fluid camera movements during tilting and panning.

- **Camera Cage:** To install extra accessories like lights, monitors, or microphones, think about getting a camera cage. The cage acts as a strong casing for your camera and offers more mounting locations so you may add accessories without worrying about breaking the camera's body.

- **Spare Batteries and Charger:** Despite the Nikon Z50 II's lengthy battery life, prolonged shooting sessions will need extra batteries. It also helps to increase steadiness while shooting handheld. You may avoid losing important pictures because of a dead battery by keeping extra rechargeable batteries on available. To ensure that you are ready for a full day of photography, an external battery charger also enables you to charge many batteries simultaneously.

- **Memory Cards:** To capture smooth, high-quality video, the Z50 II's video recording features need a fast SD card. Select a card with fast write speeds, especially if you want to record long video clips or shoot in 4K. Reliable choices that provide speed and capacity for large files are the SanDisk Extreme Pro and Lexar Professional cards.

- **Lens Filters for Particular Effects:** To balance the exposure between the dark ground and the bright sky in landscape photography, use graded ND filters. As an alternative, a star filter may provide beautiful bokeh effects that give your nighttime photos a surreal, theatrical feel.

CHAPTER SEVEN
ABOUT MAINTENANCE AND DEBUGGING

How to Maintain and Clean Your Camera

1. **Make sure the camera body is clean:** Over time, dust, dirt, and oils from your hands may collect on the body of your camera, particularly if you're shooting outside or in dusty environments. Maintaining the camera's condition and ensuring that all of the buttons, dials, and ports work properly may be achieved with routine cleaning.

A soft brush, a blower (which resembles a little air pump), a soft microfiber cloth, and an optional lens cleaning solution are needed.

Instructions for Cleaning:

+ To clean the camera, simply wipe it down with a dry microfiber cloth. Dust, fingerprints, and other surface impurities may be eliminated in this way. Because microfiber is soft, it won't damage the surface of the camera.

+ To get rid of dust from areas like buttons, ports, and seams where dirt collects, use an air blower. Because moisture may damage the camera, this is better than using your breath.

+ Use a small, soft brush (like a paintbrush) to clean dirt from buttons and cracks. Take care to avoid damaging any parts.

+ You may use a lens cleaning solution to gently moisten your towel if the camera has any sticky residue (such oils from your fingers). Steer clear of applying too much liquid since it might go into the camera.

2. **Make sure the lens is clean:** One of the most important parts of the camera is the lens. Keeping the lens clean is essential since any smudges or particles may drastically lower picture quality.

Lens cleaning solution, a microfiber cloth, a blower, and a lens brush are necessary.

Instructions for Cleaning:

+ Before cleaning the lens, use a blower to get rid of any loose debris or dust. By doing this, you may avoid getting dirt on the lens.

+ Use a tiny lens brush to gently sweep away stubborn dust.

+ Use a microfiber cloth moistened with lens cleaning solution to gently wipe lenses in a circular motion. Always start in the center and work your way out. This lessens the chance of damaging the lens and avoids streaks.

3. **The picture sensor is being cleaned:** The heart of your camera is the sensor. It is in charge of taking your pictures, thus maintaining its cleanliness is essential. Be

careful, however, since this is a fragile component. Unless you are certain that the dust or stains on your photos are due to the sensor itself, don't clean the sensor.

Instructions for Cleaning:

- The "sensor cleaning" option on the Nikon Z50 II camera menu shakes the sensor to get rid of dust. This is the first thing you should attempt before doing any actual cleaning.
- Turn off the camera and gently blow air on the sensor if the shaking is ineffective. Compressed air canisters should not be used since they may harm moisture and blow chilly air.
- If dust continues to accumulate or you are not certain that you can clean the camera's sensors on your own, professional cleaning is advised.

4. **How to Take Care of the LCD Screen:** The LCD screen of your camera is delicate, and frequent handling and cleaning may cause scratches and smudges. Maintaining the screen will help your camera maintain its visual attractiveness while also enhancing the sharpness of your photos and videos.

Requirements: Screen protectors or a microfiber cloth (the same kind used for the body and lens).

Instructions for Cleaning:

- Use a fresh microfiber towel to gently wipe the screen. Steer clear of employing powerful chemicals or solutions that weren't made especially for electronics.
- To avoid smudges, scratches, and unintentional drops, think about using a screen protector.

5. **Taking Care of the Memory Card and Battery:** The memory cards and batteries of your camera are essential for photography. They may deteriorate the camera's performance if not properly maintained, leading to erratic functioning or lost images.

Battery Maintenance:

Charge the camera's battery on a regular basis. Do not leave it uncharged for too long. The Z50 II's lithium-ion batteries, for example, dislike being kept at very low or high charges for prolonged periods of time.

- Take out the camera's battery and store it somewhere dry and cold while not in use.
- Use a dry microfiber cloth to clean the contacts on your camera. Dust might interfere with functionality and charging.

Cards for memory:

- To prevent damaging the contents, do not remove the memory card while the camera is writing data.

- Use a dry microfiber cloth to carefully wipe the card contacts clean. Avoid using liquids.

6. **Protection & Storage:** Keeping your camera in excellent condition while not in use requires proper storage.
- To keep your Nikon Z50 II safe from scratches, bumps, and moisture, put it in a padded camera case. Your lenses, batteries, and memory cards will stay safe and organized with the aid of a good camera bag.
- In order to avoid moisture damage, keep devices dry. Use a rain cover for the camera if it's going to be raining or humid, or try to avoid shooting in wet conditions altogether. Use a soft towel to completely dry the camera after using it in such circumstances.
- Keep it out of heated environments, such your automobile, since this might damage the batteries and electronics.

7. **Frequent examinations:** It's a good idea to get your camera inspected by a professional once in a while, much as you would take your car to a mechanic for routine maintenance. It could be time for a thorough cleaning or service if you're having strange issues or your performance has declined. Having the camera inspected by a specialist may help keep it in excellent operating condition, and Nikon provides servicing alternatives.

Troubleshooting: Typical Problems

- **The camera won't turn on: If your Nikon Z50 II won't turn on, don't freak out. Here is what you need to look for:**
  - **Examine the battery:** The most common reason a camera doesn't turn on is a dead or misplaced battery. Verify that the battery is fully charged. Remove the battery and put it back in, making sure it snaps into place, if the camera is charged but still won't turn on.
  - **Battery connections:** Problems may arise from dirty connections on the camera or battery. Carefully clean the camera and battery connections with a fresh, dry microfiber cloth. The battery may not connect correctly due to dirt and dust.
  - Verify that the power switch is fully in the "on" position. If you're in a rush, it's simple to think it's on when it's not.
- **It's not focusing on the camera: Although autofocus problems might be annoying, they can usually be resolved by looking at a few things:**
  - Verify that autofocus (AF) is selected on your camera. It's possible that you accidentally set it to manual focus (MF), which stops the camera from

focusing on its own. Press the AF/MF button on the lens or camera body to switch to autofocus.

➢ Dirt or smudges on the lens may affect autofocus. Use a blower and a microfiber cloth to remove dust and fingerprints from the lens.

➢ Among the several focus modes available on the Nikon Z50 II are single-point, dynamic-area, and face/eye recognition AF. Try changing the focus modes if your camera isn't focusing where you want it to. Depending on your preference, you may either hit the focus mode button or go through the camera's settings to do this.

➢ In low light, autofocus performance may deteriorate. Use a flashlight or lighting aid if you're shooting in low light, or go to manual focus if autofocus isn't functioning.

➢ Look around for anything that could be blocking the lens. Autofocus might be disrupted by fingers or a lens hood.

- **Neither the LCD screen nor the viewfinder showed any images:** If the viewfinder or screen seems black or blank, it's possible that you accidentally turned something off.

➢ **Verify Display Settings:** accidental button push or battery conservation may have turned the display off. There is a button on the Nikon Z50 II that allows you to switch between the LCD and the viewfinder. Press the Display button (next to the viewfinder) to switch between the two.

➢ **Sleep Mode:** The camera may have switched to power-saving mode, which turns off the screen to save energy, if it hasn't been in use. You may push any button to wake up the camera.

➢ Verify that the camera is turned on by checking the power button or dial. Because you forgot to turn the power dial, it may seem to be off at times.

- **"Lens Not Attached" or other error messages:** The screen may sometimes show error messages like "Lens not attached" or other warnings, even if the lens is installed correctly.

➢ **Verify Lens Mount:** Make sure the lens is attached to the camera body correctly. The camera will show the message "lens not attached" if it is not snapped into position. Make sure the lens locks into place after removing it and securely reattaching it.

➢ **Keep Lens Contacts Clean:** Dust or grime might make it difficult for the camera to detect the lens. The camera and lens interact via metal contacts, which should be cleaned and dried using a microfiber cloth.

- ➢ **Software Update:** Without updated software, certain lenses may not work properly with the camera. Verify whether there is a firmware update available in the camera's menu or on Nikon's website.
- 🞣 **No video will be recorded by the camera:** If the video function isn't working correctly or you can't capture video, it might be the result of a simple settings problem.
  - ➢ Verify that the camera is in video mode. You may switch between image and video modes by turning the mode dial to the video camera icon, which is usually located close to the top. Video recording will not be possible if it is in the wrong mode.
  - ➢ **SD Card Speed:** To handle the data, high-quality video recording (such 4K) can need for a quicker SD card. To effortlessly record 4K movies, the Nikon Z50 II needs SD cards certified as UHS-I U3 (Ultra-High-Speed) or V30. Replace your card with a faster one if your current one is too slow.
  - ➢ The camera won't be able to capture any more films if your memory card is full. Verify the amount of space left on your SD card, remove any unnecessary files, or swap it out for one with more usable capacity.
  - ➢ **Temperature Issues:** The camera may overheat and stop recording if you record for long periods of time or in hot conditions. Before trying again, let it cool off.
- 🞣 **Problems with image quality (low sharpness and blurry photos):** A few common errors that might result in soft or fuzzy images are as follows:
  - ➢ Photos with slow shutter speeds may be blurry, particularly in low light. To steady the camera, try adjusting the shutter speed or use a tripod.
  - ➢ Verify that your focus is on the appropriate area of the picture. Occasionally, autofocus may concentrate on an object in the background instead than the intended topic. In this case, selecting your focus point manually or using the proper focus mode might be beneficial.
  - ➢ Especially in low light, high ISO settings might deteriorate picture quality and introduce noise. Reduce the ISO as far as you can to achieve the finest images. To prevent utilizing a higher ISO while shooting in low light, consider using a tripod.
- 🞣 **Lagging or Freezing Camera:** It might be unpleasant when your camera slows down or freezes, particularly while you're shooting.
  - ➢ **Memory Card Problems:** The camera may lag or freeze due to a slow or full memory card. Either format the existing memory card in the camera or try a faster one (after backing up your data, of course).

- ➢ **Camera Settings:** Latency may result from certain settings. To improve camera responsiveness, think about turning down any of the high-performance settings you have selected (such burst mode or high ISO).
- ➢ **Restart the Camera:** Try turning the camera on and off again if it is still not responding. You may take out the memory card and battery, wait a few minutes, then put them back in and try again if it doesn't work.

Last Words of Advice

- ✦ To find hidden settings that could be creating problems, see the handbook. You may get a deeper understanding of the many settings and functionalities by consulting the Nikon Z50 II manual.
- ✦ Nikon often updates the firmware on their cameras. Updating the firmware on your camera guarantees that any issues are fixed and optimal performance.
- ✦ Get in touch with Nikon customer support if you're unable to resolve the problem after doing everything else. If additional troubleshooting is required, they may direct you to a servicing facility.

Optimization of Battery Life

When using your Nikon Z50 II, running out of power may be quite upsetting, particularly if you're in the midst of a session or traveling for work. Although the battery life of the Z50 II is sufficient for a mirrorless camera, there are a few tips you can follow to maximize each charge. **Let's examine some useful tips for prolonging the life of your battery.**

- ✦ **When not in use, turn off the camera:** Although it may seem simple, you'd be surprised at how many people leave their cameras running in between shots, particularly when they're changing lenses or getting ready for a shoot. Don't forget to turn off the camera while you're not using it. Like other mirrorless cameras, the Z50 II uses power even while you're not taking photographs, especially when the viewfinder or LCD is on.
- ✦ **Turn off the Auto Review function:** A lot of cameras are set up to automatically show the picture you just took as soon as you take it. This feature, called auto review, keeps the screen on for longer than is required, which may rapidly deplete your battery. Turn off auto review if you don't need to see every shot immediately. From the menu, choose Playback Settings and turn off Auto Image Review to do this.
- ✦ **Instead of using the LCD screen, use the viewfinder:** The Z50 II's superb electronic viewfinder (EVF) allows you to take pictures with less power

consumption than the LCD screen. Although the LCD screen is larger and simpler to use for framing, its power consumption is higher. While possible, go to the viewfinder since it uses less power, particularly while capturing still images.

- **Cut Down on the LCD Screen's Brightness:** The brightness of the LCD screen might be a major power drain while you're using it to take or analyze photographs. Turning the screen down while you're inside or in less lit areas may significantly extend battery life, despite the temptation to keep it at full brightness when you're outdoors in the sun. The camera's settings menu allows you to adjust the brightness.

- **Restrict Your Video Recording Use:** Despite the Z50 II's excellent 4K video capabilities, video recording may rapidly deplete the battery. The battery will drain much more quickly while filming for extended periods of time than when still photography is engaged. If you're filming for a long time, cut down on the duration of your video sessions or have additional batteries on hand.

- **Make use of the power-saving mode:** There is a Power Save mode on the Nikon Z50 II. In order to save battery life, this feature automatically modifies a number of settings, such as turning off autofocus while you are not actively writing or dimming the screen after a period of inactivity. To assist preserve battery life while you are not actively taking pictures, you may activate this feature in the camera's settings menu.

- **When not in use, turn off Bluetooth and Wi-Fi:** The Z50 II has Bluetooth and Wi-Fi, which are helpful for connecting to other devices and exchanging photos. But even when you're not using them, these features may drain your battery since they're always searching for connections. Turn off Bluetooth and Wi-Fi from the camera's menu if you don't need them.

- **Don't use Flash unless absolutely required:** Using the external or built-in flashes may significantly drain your battery. Flashes use a lot of electricity, particularly when they are fired quickly one after the other. Try adjusting your ISO or switching to a fast lens in place of a flash if you're shooting inside or at night. Make careful to use Flash sparingly if you must.

- **Always have extra batteries on hand:** Despite all of these optimization strategies, there will still be times when battery depletion is unavoidable. Having additional batteries on hand is the simplest way to handle this. The compact and portable EN-EL25 rechargeable lithium-ion battery powers the Nikon Z50 II. You may prevent a power outage by carrying one or two extra batteries in your camera bag, particularly while traveling or on lengthy assignments.

- **Utilize a Power Bank for On-the-Go Charging:** A portable power bank is an additional choice if you want to spend a lot of time in the outdoors and don't want to carry a lot of spare batteries. With the Z50 II's USB-C charging capability, you can plug it into a power bank to replenish the battery between shots. On long treks or at gatherings without power outlets, this is really useful.

- **Change to a Mechanical Shutter:** The electronic shutter might deplete your battery more quickly if you're shooting in an area with consistent illumination, such indoors. Mechanical shutters need less power, while electronic shutters are better for silent photography and faster shutter speeds. Using a mechanical shutter may help you conserve battery life if you don't mind the shutter's sound or if you want faster burst rates.

Bonus Advice: Check the Health of the Battery

Older batteries will not hold as much charge as newer ones since batteries degrade with time. It could be time to change your camera's battery if it's much less than when it was brand-new. Always keep an eye on your battery's condition and performance.

Overheating While Recording a Video

The Nikon Z50 II may overheat while capturing video, especially at higher resolutions like 4K. Although it is inconvenient, this is a common issue with mirrorless cameras that may be resolved. You may shoot for longer lengths of time by avoiding or delaying the camera's built-in safeguards, which will automatically cease recording when it reaches a certain temperature. Let's examine the causes of overheating and preventative measures.

What Causes Overheating?

It's important to comprehend the causes of overheating before moving on to the fixes:

- It takes a lot of processing power to record in 4K or at high frame rates (like 60 frames per second). Heat is produced by the internal parts of the camera, especially the sensor and processor, which work hard to handle the data.
- Heat accumulation results from continuous video recording. Heat will still be produced by even short bursts of high-quality video, but long-term continuous recording is more likely to surpass the camera's thermal limitations.
- **Compact Camera Design:** Mirrorless cameras, such as the Nikon Z50 II, are lighter and smaller than DSLR cameras, but their tiny size limits the amount of cooling they can provide. Tiny mirrorless cameras are more prone to overheat, whereas larger cameras have more space for heat dispersion.
- Overheating may be caused by environmental causes. The camera will inherently have trouble staying cool while shooting in hot conditions or in direct sunlight.

Advice for Preventing Overheating When Recording Videos

Here are some doable ways to prevent or delay overheating while using your Nikon Z50 II to record video:

- **Make recording sessions shorter:** Avoiding recording for long periods of time at a time is one of the easiest ways to reduce overheating. Split a lengthy movie into segments of 10 to 15 minutes, and allow the camera to cool down in between shoots. Resting the Z50 II for a short while will assist avoid heat shutdown since it is not designed for prolonged video recording.

- **Make Use of Outside Power Sources:** The camera puts out a lot of effort to power the system and continue shooting videos when it is powered by its internal battery. You may reduce the strain on the internal battery and allow the camera to utilize its power more effectively and generate less heat by using an external power bank or plugging the camera into a power outlet using the USB-C charging port.
  - Consider purchasing an additional battery pack that can run your camera for extended periods of time if you're doing lengthy shoots, particularly if you're filming films. Another option is to use a phony battery that is attached to a power source, such an AC converter.

- **Reduce the settings for video recording:** Although this high resolution and frame rate put additional pressure on the camera's internal components, the Z50 II can record in 4K at up to 30 frames per second. **In order to reduce the risk of overheating:**
  - Instead of using 4K, think about recording in 1080p (Full HD). This significantly lowers CPU temperature and strain.
  - For videos that don't need a high frame rate, think about shooting at 24 or 30 frames per second rather than 60. The processing load and overheating risk are reduced by lowering the frame rate.
  - If your settings permit, lower the video bitrate. Heat dissipation may be aided by a lower bitrate as it produces smaller files and requires less processing power.

- **Maintain a Cool Camera:** Although it may seem easy, keeping your camera cool is essential to prevent overheating. What you can do is this.
  - If at all possible, place the camera in a shaded spot while shooting outdoors. Direct sunlight has the ability to rapidly raise a camera's internal temperature.
  - Employ a cooling fan for your camera: For extended video recording, you may attach a small, external camera cooling fan, which is often designed for vloggers or filmmakers. By circulating air around the camera and keeping its parts from overheating, these fans may aid in cooling it.

- ➢ Take regular breaks in a cooler spot while shooting in hot conditions, such as direct sunlight or a heated room. If at all possible, shoot in an air-conditioned or well-ventilated space since using a camera in a heated area with inadequate ventilation is a certain way to cause overheating.
- ✦ **Turn on Power-Saving Features:** Numerous power-saving features in the Z50 II may assist maximize battery use and get rid of extra heat.
  - ➢ **Turn on Auto Power Off:** The camera will turn off on its own after a certain period of inactivity. This will prevent it from running continuously while you're not actively using it or recording.
  - ➢ For video shoots, turn off unused technologies like GPS, Bluetooth, and Wi-Fi. Overheating may result from these features' consumption of power, which generates extra heat.
- ✦ **Apply an ND filter:** By enabling you to shoot at a lower ISO or faster shutter speed, an ND (Neutral Density) filter may assist you minimize the need for high processing power and heat output. By controlling how much light enters the camera, you can still get the right exposure settings without overtaxing the internal parts.
- ✦ **Update the firmware:** Nikon releases firmware updates on a regular basis that enhance camera performance. While autofocus enhancements and new features are often the main emphasis of these upgrades, some may also include modifications to aid in heat dispersion and battery management. Make sure your firmware is up to date and check for updates.

How to Handle Overheating Cameras

Your Nikon Z50 II will immediately stop recording and show a warning message if it overheats while you're shooting.
When this occurs, do the following actions:
- ✦ **Switch the camera off:** Turn off the camera right away to allow it to cool. This prevents further harm by allowing the internal parts to cool down.
- ✦ **Let the Camera Cool:** Give the camera a few minutes to cool down on its own. The components may be harmed by very high or low temperatures, so keep it out of a refrigerator or other chilly place.
- ✦ **Use a Different Battery or Power Source:** If your camera is overheating because of battery strain, you may want to replace the battery or switch to an external power source.
- ✦ **Look for Obstructions:** Verify that nothing is blocking the camera's surrounding vents or airflow. The camera retains circulation and prevents excessive heat buildup when the vents are kept clean.

When to Look for Expert Help

Although owning a Nikon Z50 II is an amazing experience, issues might arise sometimes and need professional help, just as with any complex piece of equipment. Many common issues may be resolved with regular cleaning and simple troubleshooting, but there are times when professional help is needed. You may prevent more damage and maintain your camera's optimal performance by knowing when to turn it over to a professional.

Continuous Camera Issues

When the camera exhibits issues that cannot be fixed with basic troubleshooting, it is one of the most frequent reasons to seek professional assistance. For instance, there can be an issue with the internal parts if you see that buttons or dials are no longer responsive, or if the screen or viewfinder shows blurry or non-functional images. In a similar vein, if autofocus is not working properly even in well-lit conditions or if the camera produces strange sounds like clicking or grinding, these might be signs that internal systems are malfunctioning. A expert must be seen if these issues persist and cannot be fixed by resetting or altering settings.

Physical Injuries

Accidental injury is another common reason to seek professional assistance. It is imperative that you get the camera examined if you have dropped it or if it has been in any kind of mishap. Although the outside body seems to be in decent shape, internal parts may have been damaged, especially the lens mount, which is necessary for attaching and using lenses. In addition to causing alignment problems, a damaged lens mount may potentially make it impossible for lenses to install securely. A full replacement may be necessary if the viewfinder or screen is damaged or shattered; this should be handled by a qualified technician. Similarly, to prevent long-term damage to the delicate internal parts, your camera has to be properly cleaned and repaired if it has been exposed to dust or water.

Problems with the battery and power

The camera's battery or power management system is another common problem. If your Nikon Z50 II routinely consumes power faster than anticipated or won't turn on even with a fully charged battery, there may be an internal issue. Similar to this, if your camera charges sporadically or incorrectly, it's often caused by an issue with the internal power circuitry or charging port. To reduce further irritation and ensure that the camera operates as intended, such problems need expert evaluation and repair.

Problems with Sensor and Image Quality

One of the most crucial parts of the camera is the sensor, and problems with it may significantly affect the quality of the images. A dirty or damaged sensor might be the cause of persistent spots, smudges, or odd anomalies in your photos. Although there are sensor cleaning kits available, a professional cleaning or replacement will be required if the sensor is physically damaged or the dirt cannot be removed using easy techniques. Additionally, pixelated or warped images might indicate sensor issues that need to be fixed.

Software and Firmware Issues

Rather than the hardware itself, issues might arise because of the software that controls the camera. The camera may indicate a more significant software issue if it often freezes, crashes, or performs unexpectedly. A reset or a fresh firmware installation might fix some of these problems, but more complex problems would need professional repair to properly get the camera working again.

Considerations for the Warranty

If a serious issue arises with your Nikon Z50 II, you have to use it while it's still covered under warranty. If you attempt repairs on your own or take the camera to an unapproved repair shop, the warranty may be voided and you will have to pay for the repairs out of pocket. Always get in touch with Nikon support or an authorized service facility to confirm that the repair was done properly and that your warranty is still in effect if the camera is still covered.

CHAPTER EIGHT
HINTS AND TRICKS FOR USERS OF THE NIKON Z50 II

Enhancing Battery Life

Making ensuring your camera's battery lasts as long as possible is important if you're using the Nikon Z50 II and don't want to run out of power while shooting pictures. The EN-EL25 rechargeable lithium-ion battery powers the Nikon Z50 II and provides adequate performance. To assist prolong battery life and prevent missing a shot, there are a few strategies you may use. **The following are some quick and effective methods to extend battery life:**

- **When not in use, turn off Bluetooth and Wi-Fi:** The Nikon Z50 II's Bluetooth and Wi-Fi capabilities come in handy for sharing photos and using remote control applications. These Wi-Fi features have the potential to rapidly drain your battery when you turn them on. Therefore, turn them off if you aren't using them to transmit pictures or operate your camera from a distance. Just choose the network options from the camera's menu to turn off Bluetooth and Wi-Fi. By turning these features off while not in use, you can prolong battery life and conserve electricity.

- **Instead of using the LCD screen, use the viewfinder:** Although the LCD screen is useful for taking pictures, it might drain the battery. Compared to the electronic viewfinder (EVF), the screen uses more power. The LCD may be hard to see while shooting in bright light, therefore using an EVF will give you a clearer view. Alternatively, you might use the viewfinder to save battery life. The Z50 II is a great power-saving choice because of its bright, sharp EVF. Additionally, the camera immediately changes to the EVF when you hold it up to your eye, which is simple and saves energy since you don't have to manually adjust the settings.

- **Diminished Screen Illumination:** You may preserve battery life by lowering the brightness if you must use the LCD panel. Because bright displays use more energy, dimming the brightness may have a big effect. Under display choices in the camera's menu settings, you may adjust the brightness. Just make sure it's not too bright to waste power, but yet light enough to view your topic well.

- **Disable Image Review:** An image review function on the Nikon Z50 II shows your photos instantly as soon as you take them. Even while this is helpful, taking a lot of pictures quickly will deplete your battery. You may turn off this feature if you don't need the picture to show up right away after every shoot. Find the review settings in the camera's menu and choose them.

- **Switch to Power Saving Mode:** When not in use for a prolonged period of time, the Nikon Z50 II's power-saving mode may turn the camera off automatically. This feature prevents energy waste in the event that you forget to turn off the camera between shots by configuring it to go into standby mode after a certain period of time (for example, five or ten minutes). The auto power off menu choices includes the power-saving option. Your battery may last longer if you set it to a shorter length, particularly if you shoot for longer periods of time.

- **Put the aircraft mode on:** You may not have thought of airplane mode as an additional feature that might help you save battery life. All wireless connections, including Bluetooth, Wi-Fi, and GPS (if enabled), are turned off when you go to airplane mode. For photography without any of those features, this is perfect. It's a quick way to stop the camera from using too much power for connection, which is particularly helpful in remote areas.

- **Don't use Flash unless absolutely required:** One of the most effective ways to drain the battery is to use the built-in flash on the camera. Avoid using flash until absolutely necessary since it uses a lot of electricity. Consider utilizing external flashes or lighting equipment if you must use a flash; this might be more effective and save battery life on your camera.

- **Control the Time You Spend on LCD Screens:** Your battery may be depleted if you take a lot of pictures and see the results on your LCD screen often. Think about cutting down on the time you spend analyzing your photos. Take a photo, check the exposure, and then concentrate on taking more pictures rather than continuously assessing. This contributes to battery conservation.

- **Keep extra batteries on hand:** You could still need more power even with all the modifications, especially if you're going on long shooting sessions or excursions. Keeping extra batteries on hand at all times is the greatest backup plan. Because the EN-EL25 battery used in the Nikon Z50 II is compact and light, it's easy to carry a few more in your pocket or handbag. In order to charge batteries in batches while you're gone, it's also a good idea to get an additional charger. When traveling, some external chargers also let you charge via USB, which is convenient.

- **Regularly check the battery levels:** Checking the battery level indicator on the LCD screen of your camera is one of the easiest ways to keep an eye on battery life. The Nikon Z50 II has a reliable display that shows the remaining charge. Pay attention to this, particularly if you want to shoot for a long time. It's time to swap out the battery or look for a charging solution after the percentage drops.

- **In cold weather, keep your battery warm:** Your camera battery's performance may also be hampered by cold weather. Shooting in cold conditions might cause the battery to discharge more quickly than usual. Keeping your battery warm is one way to avoid this. To keep extra batteries warm, place them near your body or in an inside pocket. Changing to a fresh, warmer battery will help you gain extra shooting time if you're out in the cold for a long period.

Advice for Photographing Sports and Wildlife

Photographing wildlife and sports can be both fulfilling and challenging. You need to be quick, accurate, and flexible enough to adjust to rapidly shifting conditions. Because of its superb picture quality, compact size, and fast focusing mechanism, the Nikon Z50 II is a great option for this kind of photography. **Here are some tips to help you take the greatest action photos of sports or animals.**

- **Employ AF-C or continuous autofocus:** The continuous focusing (AF-C) setting is necessary for photographing fast-moving subjects, including athletes in motion or animals sprinting. The camera may continually shift focus as the subject moves thanks to this mode. Wildlife and sports photographers really benefit from the Nikon Z50 II's amazing Hybrid AF technology, which follows moving objects with remarkable accuracy. To configure this, go to AF-C in the focusing mode settings. As your subject travels throughout the frame, this will help you maintain it in focus. You may also set up the focus points to follow certain areas of the image, like the player's face or an animal's eyes, for more precise focusing.

- **Make Use of a Quick Shutter Speed:** When taking pictures of fast-moving action, a quick shutter speed is necessary to prevent blur and freeze motion. 1/1000 seconds or less is a common shutter speed in wildlife and sports photography. This will make it easier to freeze motion, like an athlete leaping into the air or an animal running. Try using your Nikon Z50 II's Shutter Priority Mode (S) if you're unsure how to modify the settings. In this mode, you may choose the shutter speed and the camera will automatically adjust the aperture for the best exposure. This ensures that your rapidly moving topic seems clean and sharp.

- **Use the burst mode to shoot:** You often have a fraction of a second to get the perfect image in both sports and wildlife photography. The burst mode on the Nikon Z50 II increases your chances of getting that perfect image by allowing you to take a lot of pictures quickly. Simply press and hold the shutter button to activate burst mode. With the Z50 II's 11 frames per second shooting capability, you have plenty of chances to catch a breathtaking moment. After then, you may assess the burst and choose the best shot.

- **Adapt the ISO to Low Light Levels:** Photographing wildlife and sports usually takes place in a range of lighting conditions, from dimly lit inside spaces to bright outside situations. It could be necessary to raise the ISO level in low light conditions in order to maintain a fast shutter speed without too introducing noise into your images. Don't be scared to push the Nikon Z50 II to its limit when necessary since it handles high ISO well. Although ISO 1600 to 3200 is often a good range, you may experiment depending on the light conditions. To prevent blurry photos, balance shutter speed and ISO since higher ISO settings might produce grain.

- **Make Use of the Correct Lens:** In wildlife and sports photography, the lens you choose is crucial since it enables you to capture things quickly and from a distance. Because they let you take pictures without upsetting the animals, telephoto lenses are ideal for wildlife photography. When taking sports photos, a fast telephoto or zoom lens may help you get athletes in motion while maintaining a safe working distance. For wildlife photography, a lens with a focal length of 200mm or more is often advised. A lens with a zoom range of 70-200mm or more enables you to concentrate on subjects that move quickly while you're taking sports photos. Specifically designed for the camera's mirrorless technology, Z-mount lenses are compatible with the Nikon Z50 II. Although Z-mount lenses are usually more compact and have superior focusing performance, you may still utilize an F-mount lens with the FTZ adaptor.

- **Employ the Proper Composition:** For wildlife and sports photographers to produce dynamic, captivating shots, composition is crucial. When photographing wildlife, try to capture the subject in its natural environment, focusing on specifics like the animal's movements and interactions with its environment. A sense of place may be evoked by framing images with natural elements like mountains, trees, or water. In sports photography, pay close attention to pivotal moments—those significant action moments that tell a tale. Capturing the passion and intensity of the moment is important, regardless of whether an athlete leaps or a goal is scored. By isolating your subject from the background and creating a narrow depth of focus, wide apertures (such f/2.8 or f/4) further emphasize the movement.

- **Await the Action:** Being ahead of the game is essential for both wildlife and sports photography. One of the most crucial skills you can develop is anticipating the action. You can better time your shots if you know how the subject will behave, whether it's a football player passing or a lion about to attack. For wildlife, understanding animal behavior is crucial. When hunting, moving, or interacting with other members of their group, many animals exhibit predictable behaviors. To be ready for the shot before it happens, observe the animal's behavior. In sports, observe the players' positions and movements to make educated guesses about where the action will take place. Anticipating these times will increase your chances of capturing the perfect action photo, whether it's the quarterback getting ready to throw the ball or the soccer player poised to kick.

- **Make use of a monopod or tripod:** Both sports and wildlife photography need stability, especially when using a telephoto lens, which may be heavy and difficult to hold steady. When waiting for the ideal picture in one spot, a tripod works well for wildlife photography. If you need greater mobility, a monopod is a great choice since it provides extra stability without restricting your range of motion. A monopod is often the better choice for fast-paced sports since it lets you move quickly while still holding your camera. Using a monopod minimizes camera shaking and makes it simple to follow the action.

- **Take Note of the Feeling:** Sports and nature photography both have the power to evoke strong emotions. For wildlife, this might mean catching moments of love between animals, like a mother feeding her young or just plain force, like a predator pursuing its prey. It might be the degree of competitiveness in sports, such the determination of an athlete or the celebration when a goal is scored. When shooting sports or animals, don't only concentrate on the activity. Pay attention to the little nuances and feelings that give the scene life. These images often evoke the greatest emotions in viewers.

- **Have patience:** In wildlife and sports photography, patience is crucial. While wildlife often requires long waits for the perfect moment, sports may be erratic, with a game or match changing in an instant. Instead of rushing your shots, take your time watching, getting ready, and waiting for the ideal opportunity. In wildlife photography, hours of patiently waiting in one spot may provide the ideal snap. In sports, it might mean holding off until the action surges at the ideal time during a match or competition.

Top Techniques for Portrait and Landscape Photography

Photographing Landscapes with the Nikon Z50 II

1. **Choosing the Correct Lens**: For stunning landscape photography, a wide-angle lens is essential. With a wider field of view and more adaptability, a 14-30mm or 16-50mm zoom lens is ideal for creating panoramic photographs. With the aid of wide-angle lenses, you may capture more of the landscape, creating compositions that are vast and dramatic.

2. **Make use of a high f-stop, or narrow aperture:** Focusing on as much of the scene as possible is the goal of landscape photography. Use a small aperture,

usually f/8 to f/16, to achieve this. A small aperture increases depth of field, giving the background and foreground a crisp, detailed appearance. However, keep in mind that diffraction may sometimes occur when using extremely tight apertures (like f/22) and may soften the picture a little. To find your lens' sweet spot, try a variety of f-stop settings.

3. **Make use of a tripod**: Long exposures are sometimes required for landscape photography, particularly when photographing in low light or at dawn or sunset. Use a tripod to prevent camera shake and guarantee sharp images. Because of its small size and low weight, the Z50 II is easy to carry about and assemble on a tripod.

4. **Make use of the Golden Hour:** The golden hour, which is the first hour after dawn and the final hour before sunset, usually offers the finest light for landscape photography. The light is warmer and softer at these times, creating long, striking shadows. This gives your environment more depth and better textures.

5. **Take RAW pictures:** For the most versatility in post-processing, always shoot in RAW format. Because RAW files include more information, you may change details, exposure, and white balance without compromising picture quality.

6. **Make use of graded ND filters**: Both a bright sky and a somber foreground may be found in landscape paintings. Your exposure may be balanced with the use of a graded ND (Neutral Density) filter. By darkening the sky without altering the exposure of the ground, this tool helps you avoid overexposed skies and maintains clarity in both the image's bright and dark areas.

7. **Be mindful of the foreground:** A compelling landscape requires an interesting foreground. Trees, stones, textures, and leading lines may all provide depth to the composition and aid the viewer's eye as it moves over the picture. A strong foreground draws the viewer into the picture and communicates size.

Taking Pictures of People with the Nikon Z50 II

1. **Select the Proper Lens for Portrait Photography:** In portrait photography, the lens you choose greatly affects the appearance of your subject. For portraiture, a 50mm f/1.8 or 85mm f/1.8 lens works well since it produces a beautiful blurred background (bokeh) and a natural perspective. A narrow depth of focus, made possible by these lenses, softens the background and makes your subject stand out.

2. **Make use of a low F-stop and a wide aperture:** Use a wide aperture (f/1.8 to f/2.8) for portraiture in order to get a shallow depth of focus. By obscuring the background, you will isolate your subject and draw attention to their face. This is made possible by the Nikon Z50 II's large sensor and fast lenses.

3. **Pay attention to the eyes:** The eyes are the main subject of a portrait picture. To make sure the eyes are sharp and compelling, make sure the camera is focused on them, especially the near eye. Taking crisp, detailed portraits is made possible by the Z50 II's eye-detection autofocus, which automatically locks focus on your subject's eyes.

4. **Be mindful of the lighting**: One of the most important elements of portrait photography is lighting. Since natural light is usually the finest, think about taking pictures outdoors or next to windows. In the early morning or late afternoon, the soft, diffused light creates pleasing skin tones and shadows. Steer clear of the bright midday light since it might create unsightly shadows on the face. You have more control over lighting when you utilize reflectors to bounce light onto your subject, which evens out the tone and smoothes out shadows. Using a softbox or off-camera flash is an additional choice if you're shooting inside or at night.

5. **Posing and composition:** Posing and composition have a big influence on how well your shot turns out. For a more dramatic photo, think about positioning your subject off-center according to the rule of thirds. To create more suspense, have your subject look at a little angle or swivel their head instead of straight at the camera. Steer clear of awkward and inflexible positions. Your subject should be encouraged to unwind and move freely. Generally speaking, genuine, unplanned emotions work better than heavily staged ones.

6. **Take RAW pictures**: Like landscapes, portraits benefit from RAW format since it enables more post-processing adjustments. This is particularly helpful for adjusting exposure, recovering details in highlights or shadows, and adjusting skin tones.

7. **For artistic effects, use backlighting:** If you are shooting outside, try experimenting with backlighting to create a soft, glowing appearance around your subject. A beautiful rim light or halo effect may be produced by backlighting, which gives your subject dimension and helps it stand out from the backdrop. Make sure your subject is properly exposed if you're using backlighting by adjusting the camera's settings or by reflecting light back onto their face using a reflector.

8. **Think about the background**: While you want your subject to be the focal point of your image, you also need to focus on the backdrop. Make sure it enhances rather than diminishes the topic. While a busy backdrop may draw attention away from your subject's face, a simple, clean background may assist maintain focus.

Secrets of Low-Light Photography

+ **Use a low f-stop, or wide aperture:** To catch as much light as possible, a wide aperture (low f-stop number, such f/1.8, f/2.8, or f/4) is needed. You can photograph in low light conditions without significantly raising your ISO since the bigger the aperture, the lighter enters the camera. This reduces the possibility of noise (graininess) and helps maintain picture quality. For instance, using a 50mm f/1.8 or 24mm f/1.4 lens will provide you more light-gathering power, enabling you to take crisper, brighter pictures in low light. You may easily choose a fast lens that suits your needs since the Nikon Z50 II works with a wide variety of them.

+ **Raise the ISO Sensitivity:** The ISO setting regulates the camera's sensor's sensitivity to light. You will often need to increase the ISO to make up for the lack of natural light in low light conditions. But keep in mind that higher ISO settings might add noise, giving the picture a grainy appearance. In the majority of low-light conditions, you may comfortably increase the ISO on the Nikon Z50 II to 1600 or even 3200 without producing a lot of visible noise. Never be scared to raise the ISO to 6400 or 12800 if you're shooting in poor light or at night, but be sure to check for noise in post-processing. Think about modifying both your ISO and aperture to reduce excessive noise while maintaining appropriate exposure.

+ **Reduce the Shutter Speed:** Generally speaking, you may use a slower shutter speed in low light to allow more light to enter the camera. For indoor or nighttime shots, for instance, a shutter speed of 1/30 sec or less may be sufficient without requiring significant ISO adjustment. Slower shutter speeds, on the other hand, may generate motion blur, especially when photographing moving objects or with unstable hands. You can get around this by using a tripod or by setting your camera on a stable surface or leaning it against a wall. For static or portrait situations, slow shutter speeds will allow for enough of light while maintaining sharp images. Just use caution while photographing subjects that move quickly since you run the danger of blurring them.

+ **Take RAW pictures:** You have the most post-processing flexibility when you shoot in RAW format. Unlike JPEG files, RAW files include all of the information gathered by the camera sensor, allowing you to easily adjust exposure, white balance, and restore details in the highlights and shadows. When taking pictures in low light, this is incredibly helpful. You can brighten an underexposed (too dark) photograph without sacrificing detail or introducing excessive noise. You may fully use the RAW format to edit your photos later since the Nikon Z50 II has a high dynamic range.

- **Employ stability or a tripod:** One of the best tools for taking sharp, crisp pictures in low light is a tripod. With a tripod, you can eliminate camera shaking and utilize slower shutter speeds, which is especially helpful in low light. Try to rest your camera on a table, wall, or fence if you don't have a tripod. Additionally, the Nikon Z50 II has in-body image stabilization (IBIS), which reduces camera shaking while taking handheld photos, especially at slower shutter speeds. IBIS is quite helpful in many situations where a tripod is not an option, even if it cannot replace a tripod for really low-light photos.

- **Benefit from Long Exposure Photographing:** A great way to get very beautiful low-light images is via long exposure photography. In order to capture as much light as possible, this method involves using very slow shutter speeds (from a few seconds to minutes). Nightscapes, city lights, and light trails (like car headlights) all benefit greatly from long exposure. To prevent overexposing your picture during long exposures, you may use neutral density filters (ND filters) to cut down on the quantity of light that enters the camera. For long exposure lengths, even the slightest movement might cause blur in these photos, so don't forget to use a tripod.

- **Utilize the High ISO Performance of the Nikon Z50 II:** The Nikon Z50 II's exceptional high ISO performance is one of its noteworthy features. The camera's APS-C sensor retains excellent noise reduction even at higher ISOs. The Z50 II does a better job of preserving minute details without introducing excessive grain, while other cameras have trouble with noticeable noise at high ISO. This allows you to preserve picture quality while using higher ISO settings in low light conditions. For instance, ISO 3200 or 6400 may still provide crisp, high-clarity images, which makes them perfect for nighttime or poorly light environments.

- **Utilize the Electronic Viewfinder (EVF) on Your Camera:** The electronic viewfinder (EVF) of the Nikon Z50 II is quite helpful in low light conditions. The EVF shows the exposure in real time, unlike an optical viewfinder, so you can determine if the picture is overexposed or too dark before you hit the shutter. By illuminating the environment and enabling you to see more details even in very low light, the EVF may also help you frame your image more effectively. This makes framing easier and ensures you get the image you want without having to guess.

- **Employ Focus Peaking or Manual Focus:** Autofocus may have trouble focusing on a subject in low light, particularly if the background is extremely black or lacking contrast. Changing to manual focus might let you have more control over the photo in certain situations. Focus peaking in the Nikon Z50 II makes it simple to manually adjust the focus, even in low light, by highlighting the areas of the picture that are in focus. By turning on the focus peaking option in the camera's settings, you can see exactly where your focus is, which makes taking crisp pictures easier.

+ **Adopt Night Photography Methods:** You should be aware of a few additional tactics if you're taking pictures at night. Use a wide aperture (f/2.8 or below), a high ISO (about 3200), and a long exposure (around 15 to 20 seconds) for star photography or Milky Way photos. Light painting, which uses a flashlight or other light source to "paint" portions of the image while the camera is exposed for a few seconds, is another intriguing technique to try at night. Your low-light photos may have dramatic, intriguing effects as a consequence.

Suggested Camera Configurations for Various Situations

+ **Photographing Landscapes:** Controlling your exposure and aperture is essential when taking landscape photos since you usually want crisp details across the frame. **Configuration:**
  - ➢ **Mode:** Priority Aperture (A)
  - ➢ **Aperture (f-stop):** f/8 to f/16 – A narrower aperture ensures that the background and foreground are in focus by offering greater depth of field.
  - ➢ **ISO:** 100 to 400: To minimize noise and preserve the highest possible picture quality, keep the ISO as low as possible. ISO 100 works best throughout the day.
  - ➢ **Shutter Speed:** Make sure the shutter speed is quick enough to prevent camera shaking, since the camera will set it for you in Aperture Priority mode. For slower speeds, use a tripod, although generally, 1/100 sec or quicker will work fine.
  - ➢ **Focus:** For the best results, use manual focus or position the focus point in the center of the image.
  - ➢ **White Balance:** Depending on the time of day and the atmosphere you like to create, either daylight or cloudy.
  - ➢ The RAW file format allows for the greatest amount of post-processing freedom, particularly with regard to color, exposure, and dynamic range.
+ **Photography of Portraits:** Sharp focus on the subject, especially the eyes, and a narrow depth of field are usually advantageous for portraits. Soft, attractive lighting is another something you'll want. **Configuration:**
  - ➢ **Mode:** Priority Aperture (A)

- ➤ **Aperture (f-stop):** f/1.8 to f/2.8 — A wide aperture produces bokeh, or a blurred backdrop, which highlights and isolates your subject.
- ➤ **ISO:** 100 to 800: If you're shooting in poor light, you may go higher, but a low ISO will reduce noise and guarantee high-quality skin tones.
- ➤ **Shutter Speed:** The camera will manage this in Aperture Priority mode, but to prevent motion blur in portraits, aim to keep it above 1/100 sec.
- ➤ For the best focus on the subject's eyes, use Eye-Detection AF.
- ➤ **White Balance:** Cloudy or Auto: Modify to guarantee that the skin tones are pleasing and natural.
- ➤ **File Format: RAW** - RAW files provide more freedom to modify skin tones and exposure when editing.

- ✦ **Action or Sports Photography:** Fast shutter speeds are necessary for action or sports photography in order to capture motion while keeping the subject sharp. Configuration:
  - ➤ Shutter Priority (S) is the mode.
  - ➤ **Shutter Speed:** 1/1000 sec or more — a quick shutter speed can assist capture blur-free images of moving objects.
  - ➤ The aperture, often known as the f-stop, should be adjusted to f/2.8 to f/5.6 based on the illumination. More light may be captured while keeping the shutter speed quick with a larger aperture.
  - ➤ To compensate for quick shutter rates in low-light conditions (such as indoor sports), raise the ISO from 400 to 1600.
  - ➤ **Focus:** To track moving objects, use Continuous Autofocus (AF-C) in either 9-point or 21-point autofocus mode.
  - ➤ **White Balance:** Auto or Daylight: Adjust the white balance according to the event's lighting circumstances.
  - ➤ **File Format:** RAW vs. JPEG: RAW allows you more post-processing versatility, while JPEG may be quicker if you need results quickly, particularly in hectic settings.

- ✦ **Photography in low light or at night:** To prevent noise and blur, you must carefully adjust your exposure settings while taking pictures in low light. Configuration:
  - ➤ Manual Mode (M) is the mode.
  - ➤ **Shutter Speed:** 10 to 30 seconds — for nighttime cityscapes or stars, use a long exposure to catch as much light as possible.
  - ➤ The f-stop, or aperture, ranges from f/2.8 to f/5.6. A wide aperture lets in more light, but you can change it to get the look you desire (lower apertures will concentrate more of the picture, for example).

- ➤ **ISO:** 800 to 3200: Lower the ISO as much as you can to cut down on noise, but raise it as needed to get the right exposure.
- ➤ **Focus:** Live view focus or manual focus: It's preferable to manually focus since autofocus performs poorly in low light. Focus on an item using a flashlight, and then lock it in place by switching to manual focus.
- ➤ **White Balance:** Auto or Tungsten: Use Tungsten for cooler tones if you're photographing artificial illumination or city lights, or keep it on Auto for more natural hues.
- ➤ **File Format:** RAW — RAW is the best option since night images sometimes need post-processing tweaks to restore information from highlights and shadows.
- ♣ **Photography at Macro Scale:** You may capture exquisite details of small things using macro photography, which requires exact control over focus and depth of field. Configuration:
  - ➤ **Mode:** Priority Aperture (A)
  - ➤ **Aperture (f-stop):** f/8 to f/16 — A higher f-stop will help you concentrate on the whole subject. Experiment with these settings, however, since a really high aperture (such as f/22) may create diffraction.
  - ➤ **ISO:** 100 to 800: For macro photos taken inside, you may raise the ISO a little bit, but keep it low to prevent noise.
  - ➤ The shutter speed will be automatically adjusted by the camera, but make sure it's quick enough to prevent blur from movement.
  - ➤ **Focus:** For exact control, use manual focus, particularly when taking pictures of little objects.
  - ➤ **White Balance:** Auto or Daylight: Select a setting that guarantees the subject's colors are true.
  - ➤ **File Format:** RAW: This gives you more freedom to tweak the finer details and change the exposure if needed.
- ♣ **Photographing events, such as weddings and parties:** Since you'll probably be taking pictures in a range of lighting settings and capturing ephemeral moments, event photography demands adaptability. Configuration:
  - ➤ The mode may be either Shutter Priority (S) or Aperture Priority (A).
  - ➤ The f-stop, or aperture, ranges from f/2.8 to f/5.6. A wide aperture lets in more light and blurs the backdrop, which helps you focus on your subject.
  - ➤ **ISO:** 800 to 1600: Since events often happen inside or in poorly light spaces, a moderate ISO is necessary to get well-exposed photos with little noise.
  - ➤ **Shutter Speed:** 1/160 seconds or more — to avoid blurring movement during indoor events, use a little quicker shutter speed.

- ➢ **Focus:** Wide-area AF mode and Continuous Autofocus (AF-C) monitor moving objects to guarantee crisp focus.
- ➢ **White Balance:** Auto or Tungsten: Adapt to the lighting conditions, while Auto is usually enough.
- ➢ **File Format:** RAW or JPEG: RAW offers you greater editing freedom, but JPEG can be preferable if you need to send photographs fast.
- ✦ **Photographing Travel:** You need settings that are adaptable to different lighting situations while traveling, such as bright, sunny days or softly illuminated interior scenes. Configuration:
  - ➢ Mode: Program Mode (P) or Aperture Priority (A)
  - ➢ The f/5.6 to f/8 aperture (f-stop) range offers a decent depth of field balance for both close-up and wide-scenes photography.
  - ➢ **ISO:** 100 to 800: Lower it for photos taken in the daytime and raise it for photos taken indoors or in low light.
  - ➢ **Shutter Speed:** When the camera is in Aperture Priority mode, it will choose this; nevertheless, make sure it is quick enough (at least 1/200 sec) to prevent motion blur.
  - ➢ Depending on the subject and situation, the focus may be either Wide-area AF or Single Autofocus (AF-S).
  - ➢ **White Balance: Auto:** This feature is very useful while shooting in a variety of settings since it adjusts effectively to changing lighting conditions.
  - ➢ **File Format:** RAW: RAW allows you to edit your photos in a variety of ways, which is extremely useful when working with different lighting circumstances.

FINAL SUMMARY

With its combination of portability, small size, and state-of-the-art technology, the Nikon Z50 II is a potent tool for both novice and experienced photographers. I have examined how the camera's user-friendly UI, remarkable focusing system, and excellent photographic qualities may improve your photography and filming throughout this tutorial. The Z50 II offers the versatility and accuracy you want, whether you're shooting breathtaking vistas, swift-moving objects, or dramatic movies. You may fully use your Z50 II and get results on par with those of a professional by learning the settings and functions covered in this book. Remember to try new things and use the camera's creative modes; they provide chances to improve your work quickly and easily. More than simply a camera, the Nikon Z50 II offers a starting point for your artistic endeavors. Continue honing your talents, trying new things, and practicing as you go. The possibilities are limitless if you have the correct information, resources, and attitude. Have fun shooting!

INDEX

www.ingramcontent.com/pod-product-compliance
Lightning Source LLC
LaVergne TN
LVHW060122070326
832902LV00019B/3084